ASMR:
The Sleep Revolution

BENJAMIN NICHOLLS

FOREWORD: DR.RICHARD

© Copyright Benjamin Nicholls

All rights reserved. No part of this publication may be reproduced, stored in or introduced into a retrieval system, or transmitted, in any form, or by any means (electronic, mechanical, photocopying, recording or otherwise) without prior written permission of the publisher.

The right of Benjamin Nicholls to be identified as the author of this work has been asserted by him in accordance with the Copyright, Designs and Patents Act 1988.

This book is sold subject to the condition that it shall not, by way of trade or otherwise, be lent, resold, hired out, or otherwise circulated without the publisher's prior consent in any form of binding or cover other than that it in which it is published and without a similar condition including this condition being imposed on the subsequent purchaser.

CONTENTS

FOREWORD	7
INTRODUCTION	11
PART 1 - ASMR UNKNOWN	17
Sleep: The Neglected Necessity	19
Autonomous Sensory Meridian Response?	39
Genesis	73
PART 2 - THE FELLOWSHIP OF THE TINGLES	93
Finding a Platform	95
Growing Pains: A Storm of Scepticism	133
The Long Goodbye . . .	161
ASMR Stories	167
Becoming a Whisperer	173

References	179
Acknowledgments	183
The Author	184

Dedicated to my mother and father – my source of unwavering encouragement

BENJAMIN NICHOLLS

FOREWORD

We often think of sleep as something we do at the end of our day – out of exhaustion and obligation. It is the conclusion to our day. However, it may be better to view sleep as something we do at the beginning of the day – for rejuvenation and preparation. It is the foundation to our day.

In a similar way, Ben Nicholls begins your journey into autonomous sensory meridian response (ASMR) with a chapter on sleep. Understanding sleep is an important foundation for this book and for understanding ASMR.

Is ASMR just about sleep and for helping those who have trouble falling asleep? Nope. Ben follows up the sleep chapter with a tour-de-force explanation of ASMR. He explains the triggers, the biological theories, the history, the community, the controversies, and how it may be helpful for anxiety, depression, and of course, insomnia.

Fortunately, or perhaps unfortunately if you have insomnia, this book will not put you to sleep. Ben infuses the informational core of the book with personal stories, case studies, quotes, insights and perspectives. Your journey through the book will be educational an enjoyable, expanding your understanding of ASMR in a myriad of ways.

Let me also address an important question. What makes Ben Nicholls a suitable person to write a whole book about ASMR? My simple answer is that he has created over 400 ASMR videos for his YouTube channel, The ASMR Gamer. As an ASMR artist creating content for ASMR-sensitive viewers, he is on the front lines of understanding the past, present and future of ASMR.

From my perspective, the ASMR artists on YouTube were the first major 'researchers' and 'experts' about ASMR. Their videos helped to elucidate the major triggers of ASMR. The comments on their videos helped to highlight how ASMR can help people. These video artists discussed the patterns they observed between the stimuli of their videos and the responses of the viewers. Therefore, the video creators laid the early groundwork for academic researchers to further progress the understanding of ASMR.

ASMR video creators like Ben have helped to create this foundational understanding of ASMR, and furthermore, have raised the awareness and curiosity about ASMR to impressive heights. Thanks to these creators, there is now a widespread and increasing public thirst for understanding the causes and effects of

ASMR. This book will assist with quenching that thirst, but I also hope it will make you thirstier to learn more about ASMR.

I am only able to report on and respond to a small slice of this growing public fascination with ASMR on my website and through my podcasts. On a weekly basis, I am seeing new ASMR research studies initiated, new technologies arising that may help the experience of ASMR, more famous people discussing ASMR, additional artists in diverse fields incorporating ASMR into their art forms, and more people asking questions such as, 'Will ASMR ever be recommended and utilised by clinicians to treat depression, anxiety, insomnia and other disorders?'

The understanding and application of ASMR are only at the start of a very long journey. There are more questions than answers right now, which makes ASMR very interesting and exciting. Ben's challenge was to create a book that will help to launch you on that interesting and exciting journey to understanding ASMR. I hope you continue that journey when you finish this book.

Dr Craig Richard
Founder, ASMR University (www.asmru.com)
Host, ASMR University podcast

BENJAMIN NICHOLLS

INTRODUCTION

Huddled in the corner, sitting around a wooden table hallmarked with age, a friend and I were enjoying the comforts of our favourite country pub: a dark oak interior, the roaring glow of the fire and a selection of frosty ales from the surrounding area. Deep in conversation, ignoring the general hubbub of the locals, we were deliberating a myriad of topics, ranging from the abstract to our impending final exams, and where we should travel during the summer – an eclectic selection of discussion points for a Saturday evening pint.

As we drained our glasses, the tête-à-tête naturally shifted towards the neurological. My friend, an aspiring medical student, began to ask me about a previous conversation we had had a few months prior about autonomous sensory meridian response (ASMR). I had briefly spoken to him about the ASMR sensation, a booming subculture that was emerging online, and how it was transforming the lives of the sleep deprived. At the time he wasn't too interested, and the conversation only arose after discovering that I was making these ASMR videos on YouTube. Furthermore,

I didn't have the time to offer a thorough explanation, and he didn't have the inclination to hear one.

Before asking me anything, he gave context to the sudden swerve in debate. He referred to our previous discussion and how since then he had read various articles in traditional news outlets about this phenomena. He had also seen a meteoric rise in ASMR videos, such as my own, flooding YouTube. The neurological mystery piquing his interest, the question asked covered two complex and detailed facets, requiring explanations for the physiological euphoria felt through ASMR and also the culture that has amassed around it.

He asked, 'What is ASMR?'

Fortunately, he went to get the next round, affording me precious moments to plan how I would respond to a concise but immensely broad question. The detailed explanation that followed served as the inspiration for this book as ASMR is rapidly changing the relaxation landscape. Hence, this book is intended to enable people who have the need to understand the immense utility of this experience, which can otherwise be difficult to communicate in a conversation.

Can you remember a time when someone spoke in a certain way, perhaps it was their accent or dialect, which left you feeling relaxingly entranced? Or a brief physical touch that sent a warm, fuzzy tingling sensation down your scalp? If you can, then what you experienced was a physiological mystery that in recent years has taken the relaxation industry by storm. Those searching for relief from crippling stress are moving away from the classical methods, such as massage and yoga, towards a new, rejuvenating technique available for free at the click of a cursor. ASMR is the fastest growing genre for relaxation online, lulling millions to a peaceful sleep each night whilst combatting anxiety and insomnia.

We all desire a good night's rest, but we also surround ourselves with work, emails and a smartphone that causes an existential crisis whenever it isn't on our person. These two realities are at war with one another, each vying for our attention, be it daily lethargy or the constant deliveries to our inbox, with the deceptively innocuous pinging of our phones nearly always winning. Thus, we turn to techniques and practices that we can incorporate alongside our hectic schedules to alleviate the sleep-deprived life many of us endure. It is this 24/7, always online, burnout lifestyle that led to the discovery of an innate relaxant, quicker and easier to enjoy than other methods – ASMR.

ASMR is baffling. What causes ASMR? Can anyone practice it? Why is the science inconclusive?

Just like the conversation I had with my friend, this book is intended to answer those questions and more. The ASMR community is a bustling, vibrant one, but one that is also shrouded in intrigue and misunderstanding. The concept of sleep is well documented and understood, the same with meditation, yoga and other talents that bring about mindfulness, calmness and sleep. But not ASMR. The book in your hands is intended to help correct that.

Whether it is your first foray into ASMR, naturally curious, or your failure to be lulled to sleep by standard, lacklustre tricks, then you need to discover for yourself the ways in which ASMR is revolutionising the way that we sleep. The book is divided into two main parts: the first, ASMR Unknown, delves into our relationship with sleep, detailing the ins-and-outs of ASMR, and the long history of ASMR (this revolution has simply been lying dormant, pardon the pun); this part is intended to cover the nitty-gritty of the phenomenon, demonstrating how you can have greater control over your sleeping habits through wholly human techniques. On the surface, it may appear hopelessly convoluted, tied by biological jarring jargon, but as you will discover, the opposite is true. The science behind ASMR is conflicting to a degree; therefore, it is the experiences, depictions and testimonies that weave a richer story. The scenarios and examples drawn upon to explain the topics we are dealing with are common, everyday occurrences that you will be able to relate to.

The Fellowship of the Tingles goes beyond the sensation, peering into the community behind the ASMR movement, the ways in which ASMR is presented and enjoyed, but also the popular misinterpretations whom those unfamiliar with ASMR have voiced. The tingling relaxation-inducing sleep is the message, but the community is the vessel. The ASMR community is a group I am proud and passionate to participate in, dramatically helping the lives of many. Embarking upon this project, I have spoken to a vast array of folk who have imparted their personal stories to me, and this book is anchored to those stories. It is through the efforts of the community that you may already have come across ASMR online, perhaps have previously enjoyed an ASMR video or at least heard of these strange videos. Understanding the ASMR culture is inextricably linked to understanding ASMR itself – the community is the lifeblood of the sensation.

The ASMR journey is an amalgamation of science and heart, trial and error, mystery and eureka.

At the turning of the final page, it could inspire you to try ASMR, it may change the way you relax indefinitely, and the worst case scenario, it may even bore you to sleep – ironically.

'It's a dangerous business, Frodo, going out of your door. You step into the Road, and if you don't keep your feet, there is no knowing where you might be swept off to.'

-Bilbo Baggins

Written with the need to placate a friend, sparing him a lengthy discussion, this work is a passion project I have attempted to keep laconic in order to concisely, and entertainingly, detail a vibrant new world. Prepare yourself to uncover a vista of head tingles, cohorts of whisperers and triumphant tapping.

Once exhumed, ASMR can't be ignored.

Enjoy.

PART 1

ASMR UNKOWN

BENJAMIN NICHOLLS

CHAPTER 1

Sleep: The Neglected Necessity

The concept of sleep seems trivial; we all do it and performing it couldn't be simpler than lying down with our eyes closed. Yet, millions of people regularly struggle to sleep through the night. A healthy sleep pattern is the keystone to a healthy body. It is common knowledge that we require roughly eight hours of sleep to help us function at our peak, and a proper night's sleep consists of light, deep and rapid eye movement (REM) sleep. When you compare someone who has had a proper night's sleep to someone who performed an all-nighter, you can clearly see the impairments that the sleep deprived is burdened with, demonstrating that sleep is a necessity in our day-to-day lives. You will struggle to find someone who doesn't enjoy sleeping – whether it is the clichéd image of parents criticising adolescents for not rising until noon, or the more common guilty slamming of the snooze button on our alarm clocks, we try our best to prolong the experience. This should be of no surprise when it is averaged that we spend up to one-third of our lives asleep, meaning that for someone who lives to the age of 90, 30 of those years will be spent in slumber.

Romanticised in fiction, sleep is not a popular topic of conversation in everyday life – it appears a mundane topic for chit-chat. Thus, you may be wondering why the opening chapter of this book is dedicated to what we feel we already know. To answer simply, sleep is complex. On the face of it, as stated in the opening sentence, sleep could not seem simpler. Yet, when you delve into its purpose and why it consumes such a large part of our lives, the answer is no longer crystal clear. As such, sleep is key to understanding the rise of ASMR. As a sleep aid, ASMR has helped many with problematic sleep patterns. In fact, it has been revolutionary, but to better understand why this is so, it must first be established what the role of sleep is and why people struggle to achieve sufficient amounts.

'Enjoy the Honey Heavy Dew of Slumber'

-William Shakespeare

Restorative Sleep

Multiple theories of sleep have emerged, each attempting to explore the neurological requirement for sleep in humans. A popular theory is the notion that sleep serves as a restorative function in all cognitive creatures, claiming that through extended periods of rest and sleep, the body repairs what has been lost whilst awake. In a study in 1989, the University of Chicago conducted an experiment to test the effects of sleep deprivation. The experiment consisted of 10 rats that were subjected to total sleep deprivation. Over the course of the study, all the rats died with no anatomical cause of death evident. However, the rats physically reflected the effects of sleep deprivation, including lesions on their tails and paws and a gaunt appearance due to severe weight loss. Dehydration and starvation were ruled out due to food and water levels remaining constant. The study revealed that sleep deprivation caused immune system failure within the animals, as well as increased energy expenditure that doubled original values. The effects of these two factors on the rats were exacerbated as the duration of the experiment increased.

Granted the experiment presented the effects of extreme sleep deprivation, but it is not farfetched to draw a comparison between feeling subpar or even ill after consecutive restless nights. It logically follows that the reason we feel refreshed and proactive after a good night's sleep is because of sleep itself. During restorative sleep, according to the National Sleep Foundation, breathing slows and blood pressure drops, blood flows to the muscles and tissue whilst the human growth hormone is released. Sleep can be seen as a vital biological function, a daily MOT for the human vehicle.

Brain Plasticity Theory

A more contemporary view is the *'brain plasticity theory'*. Unlike the former theory, this theory addresses the psychological rather than the physical nature of sleep. It harbours the idea that there is a correlation between sleeping and the organisation and maintenance of the brain. Observing child development, infants and young children spend between 10–14 hours asleep. It is these early years in which critical neurological development takes place. Therefore, it could be concluded that it is during periods of REM sleep that the brain is able to consolidate and assimilate the information that it receives whilst it is awake, retaining important information and discarding what isn't useful.

In *Sleep and Brain Plasticity*, Pierre Maquet et al. (2003) argues that the act of sleeping can induce 'periods of intense cerebral activity' and suggests that sleep plays a crucial role in areas of the brain such as memory, but more elusive, dreams. The theory is given greater credence by the fact that you can witness this correlation on your own. All it takes is for you to think back to the last time you were in a class or a meeting sleep deprived. It should not be difficult to recall a distinct decrease in your ability to learn new skills or retain fresh information – we have all experienced the mental ache of being overloaded with strenuous tasks when all we want to do is crawl into a duvet cocoon.

Adaptive Theory

The aptly named *adaptive theory of sleep* abandons modern studies to support its claims for why we sleep and adopts a Darwinian approach. The theory proposes that we have evolved to conserve energy by allocating specific periods of the day for activity and inactivity. Central to this theory is the view that various species have adapted to sleep during periods where wakefulness would be hazardous. Natural selection can arguably account for this. Humans, for example, are naturally ill-equipped to survive at night regardless of the quantity of carrots consumed, and sleep, assuming it is done in safety, allows that potentially deadly period of the day to be bypassed. Look no further than the comparative sleeping habits of different animals to support this statement. Animals that have few predators, such as lions and bears, often sleep between 12–15 hours a day whereas animals with numerous predators, such as grazing animals like gazelles, sleep lighter and in smaller bursts. Then there is the whole segment of nocturnal beasts, shunning daylight to prowl in the dark.

The link between survival and sleep is not solely expressed through the threat of predators; it extends to environmental pressures. Hibernation is the process of an animal entering a dormant sleep state in which its body temperature decreases and its rate of breathing slows down. Hibernation enables the safe passing of winter, a period of time when for animals such as bears their main food supply of nuts and berries disappears. Bears and animals of a similar diet would struggle to find enough food during winter and, therefore, hibernate as a survival mechanism. The adaptive theory of sleep suggests that we are biologically driven to sleep at certain points in the day.

Which Is Right?

Disappointingly, there is no right answer. Despite the growing interest in both sleeping and dreaming, a conclusive answer has yet to be found; hence, a multitude of theories surround the topic. The understanding of sleep and its function are still largely theoretical. However, the main weaknesses of each of the three main areas this segment tackles is to allocate one prime reason to why we sleep. A common thread can be found woven through all, that thread being that sleep is a requirement for survival. The thread is not to be mistaken for the adaptive theory of sleep but is, in fact, much broader. Sleep is seen to serve a plethora of purposes, each with the function of keeping ourselves alive. So, it seems that all three theories are correct simultaneously. In order for humans to flourish, we need to adapt to our surroundings, restore what is lost during daily life, and develop mentally.

What Stops Us from Sleeping?

ASMR has altered our relationship with 'circadian rhythms', our internal body clock that leads us to feel sleepy towards darkness. Reading thus far, you are likely to share a common interest in sleep, whether you are driven by the stark success of ASMR or someone who struggles to drift off at night. What we have established is that a lack of sleep has potentially hazardous health risks attached to it. The question remains: why are people struggling to sleep? There would be little cause to write this book if people were not struggling to do so – the need to engage in ASMR would be nullified. In the modern age, sleep is interrupted by various factors, some of which are self-inflicted whilst others are passive. As the ASMR phenomenon has erupted in recent years, the compulsion to search for the feeling must come from, in part, the epidemic facing the 21st century sleeper.

'Sleep is the Golden Chain that binds Health and our Bodies together'

-Thomas Dekker

Blue Light

The digital revolution has truly taken place. We check our phones over 150 times, Facebook over 20 and send emails frequently throughout a single day. We cannot escape the allure of tech, no matter how hard we try. It has formed a symbiotic relationship with us; at work or at home, even commuting, we constantly have access to smartphones or computers, connecting us to the outside world and presenting countless opportunities. People will queue for hours, often days, for Apple's latest product whilst the video-game industry alone grossed $91 billion in 2015. Humanity is intoxicated. For better or for worse is not what is to be discussed; instead, the focus is on the effects that this unprecedented level of exposure to technology has on our sleep patterns.

Blue light is emitted by electronics and energy efficient lightbulbs when in use. The light suppresses the release of melatonin, the hormone that anticipates the daily onset of darkness and prepares the body for sleep. Ever wondered why you start to yawn at sunset? Thank melatonin. In 2012, the Harvard Medical School published a paper titled *'Blue Light has a Dark Side'*. The researchers conducted an experiment comparing the effects of exposure to blue light and green light (literally the colour green that is reflected into the eyes) over a period of six and a half hours. The results were distressing: blue light delayed the release of melatonin for about twice as long as the green light and shifted the circadian rhythms by twice as much (three hours vs. one and a half). The delay in sleep following extended exposure to blue light had health problems associated with it: 'The researchers put ten people on a schedule that gradually shifted the timing of their circadian rhythms. Their blood sugar levels increased, throwing them into a pre-diabetic state, and levels of leptin, a hormone that leaves people feeling full after a meal, went down'.

As an avid tech fan – I am even writing this on a laptop – this research paper worried me. I can openly admit to starting a new show on Netflix, promising to watch just one episode, and then find myself two seasons in, losing track of time, and the sun peeping through my window – it is not my fault, blame the blue light! Ironically, the growth of ASMR as we know it is down to digital platforms, largely YouTube, which we discuss later. It is perfectly reasonable to fall asleep watching a screen, nearly all ASMR viewers do; it may just be advisable to cut down on the amount of exposure to blue light. Alternatively, you can continue binge watching content without it affecting your sleep by purchasing a pair of *Melatonin Shades*™, which are designed to filter out harmful light, or listen to ASMR audio apps and podcasts. Arianna Huffington, the author of Thrive, discussed the significant health benefits she experienced following a digital diet – restricting

digital consumption during the day and eliminating it from her nightly routine was met with decreased stress and increased mindfulness. It is incredible how our hyper-connectedness to the digital world engorges our daily life.

Caffeine Conundrum

Coffee. It has a fixed place in our daily routines, whether we drink it first thing in the morning or to bolster our spirits throughout a tiring day. Coffee, and subsequently coffee shops, have become staples of today's high streets and shopping malls, providing a convenient location to meet a friend or to work in peace. The CEO of Starbucks, Howard Schultz, describes coffee houses as 'the third place', the go to destination between home and work. Coffee as a beverage is not what causes disrupted sleep patterns; instead, it is the ingredient that coffee cravers love – caffeine. Not exclusive to the romantic imagery of roasted Arabica beans, or the waft of freshly ground coffee, caffeine is the world's most popular drug. Present in thousands of items, caffeine is consumed daily in the form of coffee, tea, chocolate and various soft drinks.

The prevalence of the drug in foodstuffs is acknowledged by the website CoffeeandHealth.org, which claims that a positive correlation exists between the daily intake of caffeine and sleep problems. As a stimulant, caffeine has the desired effect of increasing your alertness by blocking sleep-inducing chemicals, mimicking the effects of blue light (although we have been drinking coffee a lot longer than we have been playing Angry Birds). It takes around six hours for half of the caffeine to be consumed by the body and excreted; hence, a coffee in the evening often keeps you awake. The heightened alertness that you feel whilst enjoying a caffeine rush can be used to answer, in part, the effectiveness of ASMR for a large portion of people. Considering nearly everyone consumes caffeine in some form or another, it makes sense that ASMR can help those on a buzz. Discussed later in finer detail, ASMR is considered extremely effective for inducing sleep and relaxation because it creates a calm experience; it is this calm experience that can help counter the effects of caffeine and help get a person's sleep schedule back on track.

Skip the Sangria

Alcohol features heavily in society and has done so for millennia, whether drunk as a glass of wine with dinner, a cocktail while basking in the sun, or more heavily when partying. It is commonly held that alcohol, in certain amounts, can aid a person in drifting off to sleep a little easier. Look at the concept of a nightcap: similarities can be drawn between a small glass of whisky before bed and a hot drink; both provide warmth and relaxation to the body, albeit one has more of a kick. This isn't to condemn drinking; it is true that the occasional drink can help lure the sandman, and drinking within the recommended daily units is largely no cause for concern.

Unfortunately, although the last round at the bar may help you to fall asleep quicker, the overall period of sleep is poorer in quality as a result. The reasons, according to the London Sleep Centre, is because it reduces REM sleep, causes you to wake frequently in the night to use the bathroom, suppresses breathing and increases the likelihood of sleepwalking/talking. Overall, it appears that the odd standard drink has minimal effects on sleep; however, drinking in larger quantities has negative effects on your much needed shuteye. As a factor contributing to restless nights, alcohol could be seen to have a greater damaging impact on sleep than caffeine. Caffeine delays the time taken to fall asleep, but when that is achieved, the effect on REM sleep is marginal compared to alcohol, which enables sleep quicker, but the rest received deteriorates throughout the night.

Insomnia

Insomnia can be considered the crème de la crème source of sleep deprivation – it is extremely common in the ASMR community for people to suffer insomnia to some degree. Insomnia is an issue that is directly related to sleeping or lack thereof. Dr Silberman (2009), author of *The Insomnia Workbook: A Comprehensive Guide to Getting the Sleep You Need*, explains the two types of insomnia: 'Most people with insomnia have difficulty either falling asleep, known as sleep onset insomnia, or staying asleep, known as sleep maintenance insomnia'; this lack of sleep leads to increased moodiness and fatigue.

A 2011 national survey in the United States revealed that roughly one in four workers suffered from insomnia, the fallout of which led to the loss of over 252 million days of productivity each year, a growing economic concern. It is typically characterised by continuous bouts of poor quality and/or quantity of sleep. There are a multitude of causes that can trigger short- or long-term insomnia, ranging from jetlag and an uncomfortable bed to more serious conditions, such as depression or schizophrenia. A root cause for a majority of insomniacs is anxiety and depression. In *The Sleep Book*, Dr Guy Meadows (2014) comments that physiological insomnia is the 'most common form of insomnia' and that it is not related 'to any other mental or physical ill health or environmental cause'. Physiological distress contributes to insomnia by perpetuating a feeling of apprehension and dread stimulated by the interactions between your feelings and your body. Feelings of irritability and restlessness follow suit, leading to poor sleep.

A vicious cycle emerges: anxious days followed by sleepless nights leading to increased anxiety. Insomnia doesn't just affect your ability to sleep, but also your waistline; a report from the University of Leeds (2017) summarised that British adults with poor sleep patterns are more likely to be overweight, obese and have poorer metabolic health.

Insomnia isn't incurable. In many cases, it can be tackled by avoiding participation in the factors mentioned; even altering your mental outlook of sleep can reap rewards. Silberman argues that a person starts sleeping poorly because of a stressor. Then the insufficient sleep almost becomes routine because you continue to mentally fester over your sleeping problems, leading to increased tension before bed. Ultimately, this concludes with 'a conditioned physiological response that contributes to difficulties falling asleep.' Although for chronic insomnia (persisting for three or more consecutive nights), it is recommended that you seek professional medical advice.

'When you have insomnia, you're never really asleep, and you're never really awake.'

-Chuck Palahniuk

The Nap

As you can see, in our daily lives we are beleaguered by tech, food and drink, which inhibit all of us from getting a peaceful rest at the end of the day. We are unable to maximise our time in the darkness of night with sleep, insisting that we either don't need/want it. Or, we use the fact that we are restless as a natural sign that we are impervious to sleep's effects and, thus, can put it to the back of our mind. The rise in restlessness is a dangerous trend, and the fallout of which can't be ignored: the 42nd President of the United States, Bill Clinton, said, 'In my long political career, most of the mistakes I made, I made when I was too tired.' The Great British Sleep Survey (2012) found that poor sleepers are seven times more likely to feel helpless and five times more likely to feel isolated and alone. A study published in Science (2004) revealed that an extra hour of sleep does more for happiness than a $60,000 raise – sleep is a key function in reducing levels of the stress hormone cortisol, something money can't truly buy.

With the burden of sleep weighing heavily on our bodies and minds, it is clear we need to adapt our sleeping habits for the 21st century. And we have seemingly found a solution, or more accurately, a helping hand in the form of napping. A midday doze does not replace the need for eight consecutive hours of sleep; however, it does offer an opportunity to recharge when we feel ourselves flagging. According to the Pew Research Center, a third of US adults nap every day with immediate benefits. A 2015 study by the University of Michigan doctoral student, Jennifer Goldschmied, found that after waking from a one-hour nap, people were less impulsive and had greater tolerance for frustration than people who watched an hour-long nature documentary: 'Frustration tolerance is one facet of emotion regulation. I suspect sleeping gives us more distance [from an emotionally driven circumstance] — it's not just about the passing of time.'

Napping is serious business; corporations such as Uber and Google have dedicated nap installations within their headquarters – sleeping on the job isn't always a bad thing it appears. Taking a power nap, even for as short as 10 minutes during the day, can improve people's cognitive and mental abilities, but they are tricky to master. You may have experienced it for yourself. I certainly have. When you go to take a short nap, perhaps you aim for 20–30 minutes, but then awake two hours later feeling groggy with no idea what time or day it is. Of course, you could try and tackle that by using an alarm clock, but there is an argument suggesting that some have a biological predisposition to successful napping, while others wake feeling worse than before the nap. In *Biological Psychology* (2006), the author, Kimberly Cote, suggests that we 'self-select this behaviour', meaning those who nap frequently reap better results than those who nap occasionally. Research also points to how we progress through the sleep cycle reflects how well we nap; those who nap frequently often appear to be lighter sleepers, meaning they find it easier to rouse themselves. That may explain why heavier sleepers feel groggy after a nap; they slink into a deeper than intended sleep, leading to a stupefied awakening.

The act of napping is nothing new, but has steadily grown in popularity in the modern age. Those who have mastered the act of napping are seeing real benefits in their daily performance, being more active and productive at work and in their personal lives – I only wish I was one of them!

ASMR and Sleep

At the beginning of this chapter, I mentioned how in order to better understand ASMR and the popularity it has amassed, it was necessary to look at how and why people sleep. In an increasingly connected world, now more than ever it is becoming harder to rest. Writing this section, I was surprised by the extent to which our sleeping problems are self-inflicted, but worse are those that we can't help but inflict. I was further surprised by the consequences of such pitfalls and the implications they have on our day-to-day functioning. Understanding more clearly the implications of a lack of sleep, we can see that there is an intrinsic requirement to do so. The increased awareness of sleep has helped ASMR blossom, transforming the sleeping lives of thousands who find no respite in a nap, and for those who don't want to give up their cappuccinos or quit their 10-hour-long 'Mad Men' Netflix session.

Yet, what makes ASMR such a popular alternative to traditional sleep aids? Why is it drastically changing how we can approach and enjoy rest?

CHAPTER 2

Autonomous Sensory Meridian Response?

The acronym ASMR conjures either complete bewilderment or feels very familiar. Two camps emerge when discussing ASMR: one camp are those who have a partial or non-existent knowledge about what ASMR is, and on the face of it, may see it as strange; the second camp are those who recognise ASMR and understand its nuances – for them it is a little less strange. The following chapter is predominantly intended for the former camp in order to make ASMR a little less alienating. ASMR is an acronym for autonomous sensory meridian response and, fortunately, whilst the jargon is confusing, it does not take a neurosurgeon to understand it: autonomous, meaning no conscious human control; meridian, a set of pathways in the body along which vital energy is said to flow; sensory, relating to physical sensation; and response, a reaction.

In its plainest form, ASMR is a neurological response to certain visual and audio stimuli, which create an experience that is borderline euphoric. The experience itself can be characterised by a pleasurable tingling that begins in the scalp and can descend through to the neck and the spine, although the tingling is not limited to those regions – surely there is nothing strange about that!

The use of audio to promote relaxation is not exclusive to ASMR content; people have been listening to different types of audio to wrestle from the grasp of sleeplessness for centuries. Ocean sounds and classical music continue to lull many to sleep – bizarre to think that whales and Johann Sebastian Bach achieve a common goal. More interventionist methods have also been adopted. Back in 2009, the Daily Mail ran an article titled *'I'd hardly slept for 18 months': How two hours of hypnosis ended my insomnia nightmare*. The article explained how suggestive phrases could help a person enter a hypnotic trance that could be used to enter a deep sleep, although the results vary. Even before the digital distribution of music and hypnotherapy, children fell asleep to the sounds of a mother's lullaby. Unlike ASMR, it can be understood how these genres of audio are commonly accepted to help someone fall asleep; soothing, calming tones allow you to clear your head and relax. Interestingly, whilst similar calm and balmy sounds also induce ASMR, the jarring aspect for people unfamiliar with it appears to be the tingling sensation.

Triggers

Popularised by the tingling sensation, an equally vital component in experiencing ASMR is the trigger. The term was adopted by the ASMR community in reference to specific sounds or actions that, when performed, may induce a person's ASMR. The word 'trigger' perfectly articulates the feeling one feels when ASMR occurs; for those who have ever gotten a massage, or slumped on a soft bed after hard labour, experiencing ASMR is reminiscent of the instantly felt relief – velvety and soothing. There appear to be two subsets of ASMR: type A needs no stimuli and can trigger the feeling through meditation or reflecting on a triggering moment; type B is the more traditional ASMR experience requiring stimuli.

No one trigger is the same and varies from audio to visual, quiet to loud, slow to fast. ASMR triggers can be experienced in the wider world at any moment, as will be discussed. However, as those experiences are isolated from one another, I shall be focusing on recorded ASMR (also discussed further in the book) as it is the most universal. A common trigger is either whispering or speaking softly, this is the type of trigger you are most likely to be familiar with as it is often how ASMR is introduced on non-ASMR platforms. Speaking in a gentler manner naturally encourages a person to relax and to escape the rush of the world by enjoying a slower-paced style of speech. Speaking softly is a prime example; it can stir memories of childhood when you were read a bedtime story or a teacher calmly explained a lesson. Some peoples' earliest ASMR memories involve a teacher going over a question one to one, or a friend tracing a pencil over their palm. As Freudian as it sounds, I am not arguing that ASMR 'develops' as a child. I simply mean that for those who 'rediscover' ASMR, they are often brought back to those memories and how that calmness was induced.

The triggers are not exclusive to sounds with visuals also complementing the experience. Gentle hand movements are extremely prominent among the community; gently swaying hands create a calm, enclosed and comforting vibe. Other visuals are of the same ilk; more creative ASMR content involves various coloured lights slowly changing colour, moving in sedative arcs. A memory that sticks out for me was during a long car journey on the way back from holidaying in Cornwall. Cruising down the motorway at night, with the headlights softly illuminating the road ahead, the scene was rather tranquil. The gentle hum of the engine, the emptiness of the roads and the soothing rocking of the car would be met with a pleasant tingling sensation.

Common triggers, such as whispering, speaking softly, hand movements, but also the gentle thud of fingers tapping and the crinkling of plastic, are just the tip of the iceberg. Beneath the surface lies the hard-core, intense triggers. The effectiveness of them can be divisive with some swearing by them whilst others loathe the mention of their names. Supposedly, intense triggers may include lip smacking, mouth sounds (using the saliva in your mouth), chewing gum and inaudible whispering (whispering extremely quietly – well, quieter than normal whispering). Is there a neurological pleasure discrepancy? For some, it is pleasurable to hear intense triggers, whilst others can't appreciate the same sounds and respond negatively.

Interestingly, there is suggestion of a link between certain ASMR triggers and personality types, hinting that different personalities are more receptive to different triggers. A mini-survey conducted on an ASMR subreddit revealed that this maybe so. The survey looked at various personality types denoted by the Myers-Briggs theory, which assigned a letter (such as 'E') to a personality trait (such as 'Extraversion'). A person with an INTP personality is described as a logician – someone who is innovative and has a thirst for knowledge; someone with this personality claims to be triggered mostly by doctor's role plays (explored later). Another example is a person who has an ENFP personality – a creative and sociable free spirit, this person prefers ASMR videos that are less scripted and ramble-based. These preferences are logical. Perhaps the reason why triggers on par with your personality are more effective is because you become more engaged with the content – does this increased focus make you more susceptible to experiencing ASMR?

Overall, the sounds that trigger a person's ASMR is largely subjective. We know that there are commonly accepted triggers which are borne out of popularity and general effectiveness. It is entirely possible that any sound can generate an ASMR sensation, even sounds that you wouldn't necessarily associate with relaxation, let alone ASMR – the noise of a fan and white noise (a static-like sound) have been known to send people to sleep.

AScienceMR

Mystery and intrigue has given rise to speculation and criticism surrounding ASMR – to pry is to be human. It is difficult to validate ASMR as a biological reaction to certain stimuli largely because little credible scientific research has taken place. It has 'escaped the eye of scientific research', according to a 2015 report from the Department of Psychology at the University of Swansea, titled *Autonomous Sensory Meridian Response (ASMR): a flow-like mental state*. Despite amassing a 'community of thousands', no 'rigorous scientific research' has yet to be conducted. Interest in the topic thus far largely consists of various questionnaires completed by tingle enthusiasts. A slew of criticism from those who do not experience ASMR, or don't know if they experience ASMR, follows questioning the legitimacy of the feeling.

Science has yet to confirm or deny the existence of ASMR, but I am convinced that it is real beyond a shadow of a doubt. I, alongside countless others, experience ASMR; the tingling sensation in the scalp, the wave of relaxation – these hallmarks of ASMR have all happened to me. Admittedly, these claims can be disregarded at face value. The subjectivity of it all and the fact that not everyone experiences it can seem a little too convenient with people jumping on the metaphoric bandwagon for the latest fad. Assuming this is true, for what gain? A plethora of stories surface of people stumbling upon ASMR, revealing how they have experienced it their entire life and can hark back to feeling it when they were younger, but they didn't have a name for it. For myself, ASMR demonstrates a close relationship with our brain chemistry in order to trigger a neurological response like this, meaning that it is too entwined with our biology to stand by throwaway comments suggesting it is a recent human development.

Not quite as epic as the story of David and Goliath, it is difficult to convince those who do not experience ASMR that the tingling sensation is beyond illusory. Although hope is not lost. Regardless of the lack of concrete evidence to explain ASMR, multiple theories are gaining traction that refine our interpretation of the brain and potentially point towards an answer.

'Science is simply the word we use to describe a method of organizing our curiosity'

-Tim Minchin

Happy Hormone Hypothesis

A promising school of thought is Dr Richard's *happy hormone hypothesis*. The proposal focuses on four major hormones: dopamine, oxytocin, serotonin and endorphins. In layman's terms, due to myself not being a specialist in chemical connections in the brain, I will explain why the relationship of these hormones suggests that they are part of the key to unlocking the solution to ASMR.

- *Dopamine*: Traditionally considered the 'happiness drug', the hormone mediates desire in the mind and compels you to pursue experiences you desire, including food and sex; certain abusive drugs also stimulate dopamine release.
- *Oxytocin*: Dubbed the 'cuddle hormone', oxytocin is released through closeness or social bonding, including eye contact and personal attention, underpinned by an atmosphere of safety. It is widely known for its role in promoting bonding between parent and child. Oxytocin intensifies a person's memory of a relationship – if you're ever feeling cuddly around someone, odds are its oxytocin!
- *Endorphins*: Responsible for masking pain and discomfort, endorphins allow you to push through pain barriers and initiate a positive feeling in the body. They are also simply delivered to elicit

pleasure regardless of pain or injury – like during sex. Endorphins are widely associated with athletes, the term 'runner's high' relates to the endorphins released during extensive exercise. I have never run long enough to experience this elation, so I will just have to trust the sporting community.

•*Serotonin*: This hormone is responsible for controlling your general mood, with depression linked to a serotonin deficiency. Levels of 80–90% of serotonin exist within the intestines; diet, exercise and light all effect your levels of serotonin. Serotonin also plays a role in the central nervous system.

ASMR's euphoric effect could be the result of a combination of these hormones. A popular trigger for ASMR is personal attention through the creation of a comforting and friendly setting. Our understanding of oxytocin may suggest that this hormone is released during an ASMR experience, particularly ASMR videos that emphasise closeness. Dopamine release could occur by anticipating that an ASMR YouTube video will be relaxing and a response to the reward of a pleasing video. This could explain why multiple ASMR viewers watch frequent videos in succession; they are driven to recreate the ASMR feeling following a dopamine release. Endorphins might be accounted for due to the pleasurable experience that ASMR incites; nonetheless, a claim can be made. In the same paper published by the University of Swansea in 2015, 38% of the participants enduring chronic pain noticed relieved symptoms for a short time; endorphins could be seen to heighten the relaxation of ASMR by relieving pain.

The hypothesis appears promising. We know that ASMR originates within the brain, so the immense relaxation that occurs could seemingly come from a hormone release, a neurotransmitter or a combination of the two. The ambiguity remains, however, as it isn't clear why the hormones are released or if they even are; also, what exactly causes the tingling sensation – what part of the brain controls the buzz? The relationship between hormones, neurotransmitters and the brain could be a vital part of the ASMR puzzle, but not the picture as a whole.

The Misophonia Link

The term 'misophonia' was conceived by Pawel and Margaret Jastreboff in a paper published in 2000. Researching tinnitus, the couple discovered that patients reacted negatively to certain sounds and believed that 'misophonia is present when an abnormally strong reaction occurs to a sound with a specific pattern and/or meaning to an individual'. Misophonia is literally the hatred of certain sounds and is a condition where negative emotions (rage, fright, repulsion) are triggered by certain sounds, such as lip smacking, chewing and snoring – for some, not the most pleasant sounds. If you recall feeling agitated when someone was chewing obnoxiously, this is similar to what misophonics experience except to a greater degree. Misophonia is quite common; a 2014 study at the University of Florida revealed that 20% of 500 participants demonstrated symptoms, yet it is largely self-diagnosed. 'Existing' for nearly a decade longer in scientific thought than ASMR, the cause of misophonia is still blurred. Similarities can be seen between misophonia and phonophobia (an aversion to loud sounds such as fireworks, or the din of large crowds) and is considered genuine, except the root cause is still to be found.

'Chewing gum is really gross, chewing gum I hate the most'

-**Willy Wonka**

Case Study: Sallie

The case study of Sallie explains in a clearer fashion the reality of misophonia, and how, as with ASMR (albeit opposite responses), it can have a deep physiological effect. Sallie is not someone who experiences ASMR, but she suffers from the extreme irritancy of misophonia.

Unaware of the term, Sallie noticed certain noises bothered her from around the age of 12, in particular the eating of breakfast cereal and the clinking of a spoon on china. The aftermath would be leaving the table in a rage because of the effects that the sound had on her. Misophonia continued into later life, the pinnacle of which occurred in the workplace. Working in an office, the din of snacking, the slurping of coffee and tea, and the repetitive drone of keyboard typing was a real discomfort. The angst of office life partly inspired her to establish her own business in 2008, allowing Sallie to work in a quiet studio, free from the raucous hum of her previous workplace.

Fast forward to 2012. Sallie was tired of her colleagues finding her discomfort amusing and wondering why certain noises bothered her so badly – 'what on earth was wrong with me'. Googling the quite comical question, 'Is it normal to want to kill someone for eating an apple?', she came across a talk show host who revealed that she suffered from this alien term, misophonia. Sallie was finally able to identify her experiences with a name, bringing her huge relief. Scouring the internet, it emerged that there were many like herself who also suffered from misophonia – her condition wasn't isolated.

The issue remains that there is no universal treatment guaranteed to work, and with a lack of knowledge surrounding its origin, no clinical treatment is currently available. Potential respite can be found in herbal remedies. Sallie herself, motivated by the lack of options online and an interest in flower essences, developed Misocalm, which isn't a cure for misophonia but is designed to take the edge off irritancy and anger.

Efforts put into understanding ASMR focus on the experience itself, but it is possible that the answer could lay in cracking misophonia. Aside from the commonality of both being responses to audio/visual triggers, the intriguing part is that some of the triggers of misophonia are the same for ASMR. Chewing noises may enrage one but be salubrious for another. Personal blogs chronicling their experiences with misophonia reveal that some experience both sensations – a cruel double-edged sword. The link between the two is further evidence that there is an isolated part of the brain that responds to certain external stimuli, causing both a mental and a physical reaction. The more important conclusion is that if there was a specific region of the brain that served as a causal link for these two reactions, why does the same trigger evoke opposite results and why do some people not hear it at all? Questions continue to be raised, but it is obvious that these neurological responses are a reality.

Synaesthesia – Taste the Rainbow

A fascinating neurological condition called synaesthesia blurs the boundaries between the senses as the stimulation of one sense incurs the stimulation of another. It is quite possible to suggest that ASMR is a form of synaesthesia or at least birds of a feather. Colourfully portrayed as 'seeing music' or 'tasting the rainbow', those with this unique condition may report that letters in black ink are experienced in a spectrum of colour, or that musical notes leave a taste in their mouth. In *Wednesday Is Indigo Blue*, Richard E. Cytowic and David M. Eagleman (2009) writes: 'synaesthesia occurs in one in twenty people, and is even more common among artists', potentially accounting for why creative people perceive the world differently than most.

Is ASMR a subset of synaesthesia? I cannot claim that the tingling sensation I experience is particularly tasty, but there are types of synaesthesia that illicit an emotional response from typically non-emotional stimuli like ASMR. Mirror-touch synaesthesia is intriguing as it involves an individual experiencing the same sensation that another person feels. For example, someone with this condition who observes a person combing their hair would feel the same sensation. Can you think of a time when that has happened to you? I can recall times during a blazing hot summer and seeing someone quench their thirst with a drink and almost tasting the cool water myself. Synaesthesia is considered to be developmental. In the case of mirror-touch synaesthesia, in the paper *'Mirror-Touch Synaesthesia in the Phantom Limbs of Amputees'*, Aviva I. Goller et al. (2013) claim that 'following amputation, 98% of amputees report a "phantom" feeling that the missing limb still exists', and that they experience this type of synaesthesia. It suggests that, presuming we have pre-existing knowledge of what it feels like, we can re-experience that feeling in our mind.

Synaesthesia is only experienced by roughly 4.4% of the general population, which may account for why not everyone experiences ASMR. Synaesthesia is widely accepted by the scientific community; the technology is still lacking to map how it works, but a plethora of papers have been published eluding to the idea that the functioning of our senses is not as clear cut as once thought.

'The sound of colours is so definite that it would be hard to find anyone who would express bright yellow with bass notes or dark lake with treble'

-Wassily Kandinsky

? = !

At the beginning of this chapter, I mentioned that for those who had never really understood ASMR it can seem a little bizarre. Why do some brains tingle in response to certain sounds? No matter how you phrase it, the question remains strange. Hopefully, the concept of ASMR should now seem clearer. By learning how certain sounds illicit an ASMR response, it can be seen that it is as ordinary as music making someone emotional – well, kind of. The reason why it does so, annoyingly, continues to be unknown. The fog that clouds our understanding is retracting, the three possible leads discussed are all areas undergoing greater research. However, at the time of this writing, it is impossible to say when answers will emerge.

It could feel slightly underwhelming for there to be no conclusive answer. Debating the validity of the tingling sensation is problematic without credible backing. On one side, it is disparaging to the ASMR cause, but on the other, it could be seen as beneficial as it bolsters interest. The reality remains that hundreds of thousands of people claim to experience ASMR, regardless of its validity (although I argue strongly in favour of it being valid), and people inside and outside of the community participate whether through videos, blog posts or on the news. To cut it short, people are interested. In one survey alone, published on

ASMRuniversity.com in 2014, the number of respondents exceeded 20,000.

The phenomena of ASMR is not limited to its scientific origin. Knowing the basis and function of ASMR is only a piece of the pie, and it serves a greater role. If only the science was important, its influence would not be as far reaching as it is. ASMR plays a substantial role in peoples' lives morning, noon and night. The reason being because of how the tingling sensation and feelings of relaxation effect day-to-day life. Yet, what exactly are the benefits experienced by ASMR? Why do people return to ASMR videos on a daily basis?

The Draw

As an ASMR content creator, I have the opportunity to work closely with other creators, but also retain a close connection with the audience I have amassed. Speaking with both creators and respective audiences, they provided a pool of wealth in terms of diverse reasons that lead them to search for ASMR videos on a daily basis. In a sense, the following section provides the greatest indication of a typical ASMR viewer and how ASMR influences their viewing habits. It would not be wrong to say: 'people watch ASMR because it is relaxing'; this is true and to state otherwise would be to contradict the whole book. Relaxation is simple by definition, but vague in application. Ordinary people seek relaxation for a plethora of reasons: from a stressful home/work balance to general unhappiness. Relaxation accommodates all of these and ASMR, for those who view ASMR online, is claimed to do much of the same.

On a daily basis, comments like the following are received on my own channel and many others:

'Had three of the worst night's sleep of my life; your video tonight cured it.'
'When I was off work with depression, I found that videos such as yours had a massive impact in curbing my anxiety . . .'
'I am currently in the middle of exam week; I want to thank your videos for helping me focus.'

The purpose of those comments is not for an ego boost (honestly) nor to suggest that ASMR viewers are sycophants, but to demonstrate that these audiences return time and time again because they take away something positive. Think of it as a hobby; many hobbies require huge sums of time and dedication, which you do not mind providing because you get something out of it. Like anything, if it does not have a direct positive impact on our lives, we care little about it.

The benefits claimed by ASMR are multifaceted and can only be verified currently by people's testimonies at this stage . . . catch up, science! Scouring various ASMR forums and the comment sections of leading ASMR content creators, three benefits emerge as typical drivers for ASMR content besides general relaxation. ASMR is used as a study/sleep aid, reducing depression and a coping mechanism for post-traumatic stress disorder (PTSD).

Disclaimer: I am not a medical professional and I do not advocate the engagement of ASMR media at the cost of prescribed medical treatment/consultation.

'It is Health that is real Wealth and not pieces of Gold and Silver'

-Mahatma Gandhi

Midday Cramming and Midnight Snoozing

It has been established in the first portion of this book that sleep is an important part of human biology and that various factors inhibit our nightly routine. The rise of ASMR is built upon the awe stirred by the tingling sensation, but also the envy of its association with a good night's sleep. The claim is supported by the 2015 scientific paper from the University of Swansea revealing that 98% of the participants turned towards ASMR for relaxation and 82% for the purpose of sleeping.

It is not difficult to imagine struggling to get a decent night's sleep. Picture this: you are up late working or tossing and turning in your duvet thinking about tomorrow's plans. You head on to YouTube to peruse your favourite triggers, and within a few minutes, your ASMR kicks in, and you start to feel your body relax and your eyes droop. It is a familiar way to end the day for many ASMR enthusiasts. A brief word of warning: when watching ASMR videos lying on your bed, sofa, etc., be wary of the position of your device. Too many times I have been woken from a peaceful slumber as my smartphone collapses onto the bridge of my nose!

Procrastination is a problem that faces us all. Unless you possess the extreme focus of Buddhist monks, you are likely to let your mind wander occasionally while performing tasks. I could rattle off a list of distractions that want me to give them attention instead of writing these words . . . but as that would be a banal literary tool to employ, I will refrain from doing so. The point of that tangent was to emphasise how it is becoming increasingly more difficult to focus our thoughts and our efforts. For me currently, it is continuing to focus on this paragraph; for you, it could be trying to remain focussed on reading these words.

Listening to soothing sounds and repetitious triggers heightens your focus. Listened to as background accompaniment, the mind sharpens as you become accustomed to the sounds. In turn, you are able to block out interruptions, maximising the limited time you set aside for studying or to concentrate on sleep. I have used ASMR in both cases; essay deadlines are the bane of every student but was made manageable through listening to ASMR and allowed me to unclog my thoughts the night before exams.

Don't just take my word for it:

'Yes, for me ASMR does. I discovered this by listening to ASMR at work and realised it made my day go by faster and less stressful. I'm able to focus on my work with the background "white noise".'

– Anonymous

'I recently found ASMR videos on YouTube, and my life has been blessed; it makes me be more present, as this is an issue of mine, calmer, peaceful, and I can concentrate more, and I started to play it in the background while doing schoolwork as I haven't been motivated lately, and it really helps me. I love it and I'd also love to know how it affects the ADHD brain.'

– Kate

'Yes, absolutely! I've listened to various ASMR videos at work and at home doing work for school, and it really helped me concentrate! I used to get distracted by the littlest things, but no longer! I've seen myself finishing work at a faster and more efficient pace, and I've noticed that I no longer have anywhere as much anxiety when I'm working! The white noise and the relaxing tones of the videos have helped me immensely!'

– Nathan

Uplifting Your Spirits

Anxiety and depression are debilitating conditions that can leave someone bedbound. According to the World Health Organisation (WHO), 350 million people worldwide suffer from depression, and is the leading cause of disability and a leading contributor to suicide. Genetics, stress, grief and difficult life circumstances are all factors that can lead to someone experiencing anxiety and depression in their life. The corporate structure favours productivity over personnel; 24/7 attachment to smartphones and email are the traits believed necessary to reach the next rung in the business world. And it translates into the educational systems, too, dogmatically colouring examination results as the single grain that tips the scales for future success, placing children under immense pressure. With the number of sufferers so high, the range of available products to reduce the effects is unsurprising. A variety of treatments have been manufactured to help those suffering from depression, ranging from herbal remedies to chemical pharmaceuticals – in many instances, people require these to function.

Receiving emails and personal testimonies from people who suffer from anxiety and depression, my interest was piqued when they explained how ASMR helped them alleviate symptoms of these illnesses. The same scientific paper produced by the University of Swansea claimed that 80% of participants noticed a significant uptick in their overall mood. What caught my eye was the personal account attached to this figure from someone whose anxiety interrupted daily life. After a visit to the hairdresser, their pressures decreased. It is unknown if it was the gentle snipping of the blades or the casual banter between the two or even both that helped, but what was clear was the link to ASMR: 'I can only describe what I felt, like an extremely relaxed trance-like state . . . a little like how I have read perfect meditation should be but have never achieved.'

Case Study: James

The following case study is a resonating example of someone who suffers from depression and utilises ASMR as a coping mechanism. James is a viewer and friend of mine who lives a normal life for a man in his twenties. The trade he undertakes is photography with a particular passion for music; he also engages in video games, film, and is an avid supporter of Liverpool Football Club (we all have our flaws). On the face of it, there seems no obvious reason why he wouldn't be happy. Yet, it was while pursuing his love of music that sadness crept in; August 2011, whilst attending a music festival, James noticed that he was struggling to enjoy himself, with his favourite bands failing to rally his spirits. In October of that year, he was diagnosed with depression.

Depression led to a state of limbo, neither here nor there. A loss of appetite and the struggle to meet up with friends made depression feel insurmountable. Treatment began with therapy and doses of sertraline (an antidepressant). James admits that these traditional remedies helped to battle his depression, but found ASMR to be a useful supplement that was occasionally more effective. James had experienced ASMR earlier in life, fondly recalling whispering in movies and television. He began his journey to reignite this feeling by searching for whispered videos and soon became consumed by the plethora of content available. For James, ASMR allowed him to feel as if someone was directly helping him and provided an escape during stressful times. The tingly feeling emanating in his head allowed him to find sleep when it evaded him and was a source to turn to when feeling low.

Depression and anxiety are unfortunate and complex issues. The purpose of this topic is not to explicitly explain or help those experiencing these issues. Nor is it to purport ASMR as a cure-all. The reason it is mentioned is to highlight that ASMR really is used in conjunction with other methods to help serious conditions – even if the positive effects felt are short lived. The fact that even one person benefits from ASMR in this way demonstrates that the effects, or more accurately the value, is underestimated.

PTSD

PTSD is a severely upsetting disorder for sufferers. Commonly found amongst soldiers, PTSD may arise after enduring a physical or psychological trauma. Otherwise known as shellshock or war neurosis, PTSD effects people by suspending their memory flow. During the moment of a traumatic event, the mind struggles to store the memory until after the event has occurred, thereby forcing the preservation of the sights, sounds and smells.

The human psyche is delicate and whilst as a species we are robust, the mind can easily be damaged from the inside. Traumatic events come to the fore as nightmarish flashbacks, creating further distress to those vulnerable. These re-experiences can be instigated randomly or by symbolic reminders of the event. For example, those with shellshock can be distressed from loud noises such as fireworks. PTSD can cause someone to become easily startled, irritable, extremely alert and self-destructive. If symptoms are left untreated, it can develop into depression and potentially suicidal thoughts.

ASMR helps those with PTSD in much the same way as those with depression. ASMR videos help to elevate mood and calm a person down if undergoing a stressful situation/environment. A vast number of content creators make videos specifically targeted towards helping those who suffer from PTSD. The most popular of these have common themes: soft sounds, gentle hand movements and calming backgrounds, which are used to take the person's focus away from anxious thoughts.

Meditative Thought

The reference to Buddhist monks, whilst in jest, has relevance; the relationship between meditation and ASMR can be seen as analogous, not totally disparate. Meditation, the art of focusing the mind, has its origin in antiquity; Buddhist mediation is believed to have derived from India with sutras (ancient Indian texts) referencing meditative states as far back as the 1st century BCE. It is then believed to have been ferried along the Silk Road to China; tradition has it that Buddhism was introduced after the Han emperor Ming Ti had a dream about a flying golden deity that was interpreted as a vision of the Buddha. As Buddhism developed in the oriental East, so did the practice of meditation. Interestingly, meditation wasn't exclusive to the East. The ancient Roman philosopher, Plotinus, wrote about spiritual, meditative exercises in *The Enneads*, published in the third century AD. Although it did not gather support among Christian meditators of the period, meditation as a practice has been incorporated into religions such as Judeo-Christianity and Islam.

Meditation takes many forms, differing between regions and schools of thought. The version popularised in the West is Zen Buddhism, an amalgamation of Indian Mahayana Buddhism and ancient Chinese philosophy Taoism, which spread to Japan and Korea before reaching Western shores (Zen is the Japanese pronunciation of the Chinese word Ch'an; 'Ch'an' is the Chinese pronunciation of the word Dhyana in Sanskrit, translating roughly to meditation). The desired outcome for Zen meditation is to attain a deeper understanding about the meaning of life, without being misled by logical thought or cultural lexicon; meditative positions, breathing exercises and other techniques are all used to block interruptions and harness mindfulness.

The relationship between body and soul has enraptured philosophers for millennia, heavily influencing the philosophy behind meditative practice. The ancient Greek philosopher, Plato, believed the soul to be distinct, immaterial and immortal. Plato's *Phaedo* recounts Socrates' deliberation regarding the source of knowledge; through the dialogues, he explains that the body and soul must be distinct entities as we are born with a prescient awareness of the Forms – the soul is the 'ghost in the machine'. Dualism, the belief that the body and soul are separate, has been heavily countered: Aristotle rejected dualism; he held that the soul gives form to the body and can't be separated, in the same way as you can't remove a hallmark from a wax stamp; the soul actualises the potential of our body, a symbiotic existence. The very existence of the soul is even rebuked; Richard Dawkins, a biological materialist, doesn't believe in a soul, maintaining that life is simply physical matter made up of DNA. We are simply 'gene machines' driven by our genes to protect and duplicate themselves. Taking the approach that we are 'survival machines', Dawkins believes that the mind is nothing but 'a computer made of meat' – evolution filters in the desirable genes and filters out the rest.

Meditation emphasises the spiritual unity between the mind and the body, focusing the mind so that it becomes peaceful and synchronised with the body as a whole – you don't need to believe in spirituality to get something from mediation. Allowing yourself to decompress and be present, meditation has a catalogue of benefits accredited through scientific studies, including increased mental strength and resilience, heightened optimism and self-esteem, and lessened feelings of anxiety, loneliness and depression. Steve Jobs heavily implemented meditation into his life as a tool for reflection: 'If you just sit and observe, you will see how restless your mind is. If you try to calm it, it only makes it worse, but over time it does calm, and when it does, there's room to hear more subtle things – that's when your intuition starts to blossom and you start to see things more clearly and be in the present more. Your mind just slows down, and you see a tremendous expanse in the moment. You see so much more than you could see before.' Incredibly successful people attribute meditation as a factor for their success: Rupert Murdoch, Oprah Winfrey and Yoko Ono, to name a few, use it to clear their minds and connect with themselves, the world and even the Divine.

The symptomatic mirroring between meditation and ASMR is fascinating. Accompanied by the euphoria in an ASMR experience is a sense of stillness, a feeling of calm awareness. Whilst more transitory than the effects of prolonged meditation sessions, ASMR mimics the benefits of meditation, including those health-related. The next time you hop onto a yoga mat to meditate, try plugging in some headphones and experiment. You may be pleasantly surprised at the effectiveness of ASMR – who knows, in the future, we may have ASMR centres popping up, overshadowing the meditation market!

The shared philosophy between the two is the necessity to take care of your mental state, not just your body. In a world ravished with stress, burning-out is driving up preventable ailments. Just as you would go to the gym to care for your body, allow yourself unfettered mental breathing space to empty your mind.

> *'When you arise in the morning, think of what a precious privilege it is to be alive – to Breathe, to Think, to Enjoy, to Love'*
>
> -Marcus Aurelius

Viva La Revolución

ASMR is revolutionising the way many individuals sleep, relax and consume entertainment. People are turning to ASMR content daily to positively influence their lives, help them work, cope with ailments and simply unwind. Revolution is the only word for it. Never before since meditation has there been a method for relaxation that transcends countries and cultures so seamlessly and rapidly; the digital age has allowed for the augmentation of ASMR in a short period of time. ASMR is an intrinsic, potential alternative to over-the-counter sleep aids to be used whenever a person desires in the quantity of their choosing. We do not know why some of us tingle and some do not, what triggers people and what does not, but we do know that when we do trigger our ASMR, benefits ensue.

The question yet to be answered is: when did it all begin?

CHAPTER 3

Genesis

Up until now, we have only referred to ASMR in a present sense. With all the debate on hormones and triggers, it is necessary to acknowledge the history of ASMR in order to appreciate the way it has manifested itself today. The history of any particular topic, be it the 16th century English Reformation or the last days of Caligula, allows us to contextualise past events, people and cultures that have shaped the present and undoubtedly the future. Chronicling ASMR may prove more difficult than researching the battle of the Somme, as there is less tangible evidence to evaluate. As a neurological sensation, it could reasonably be assumed that ASMR spans almost the entirety of human history. ASMR could be considered to have been 'around' in ancient civilisations such as Rome and Egypt. Haircuts, a known trigger, were mainstream in these cultures; for example, in Egypt, hair was usually maintained at shoulder length – Cleopatra had to win Mark Antony somehow, if hegemony over the Nile wasn't enough.

Ancient fashion is not the concern of this chapter, but as haircuts are known to trigger people, there is a strong argument to suggest that ASMR occurred in ancient times. Certainty, however, is not guaranteed as we have yet to confirm what in our brain induces ASMR and if that faculty existed at the same time. If, for a moment, we considered that it is the same (a plausible presumption), natural triggers, such as whispering, potentially dates ASMR back to the birth of humanity, revealing that the history of ASMR is symbiotic with our own. The biological history of ASMR is incoherent, and dedicating a chapter to 'maybes' would be worthy of little merit. Instead, the following focuses on the rise of ASMR as a term and the content that catalysed its discovery.

> *'History is a Greek word which means,*
> *literally, just Investigation'*
>
> **-Arnold Toynbee**

1980s

We start our history in the 1980s, a decade that saw Duran Duran storm the music world, Nintendo captivate the electronic world with their plump pixelated plumber, and the DeLorean DMC-12 sports car grace the motoring world – it was an era of creative innovation. The golden age of digital progress was played out against the backdrop of political turmoil: the United Kingdom endured miners' strikes during the controversial Thatcher premiership; Nelson Mandela continued to fight against apartheid in South Africa; and the United States experienced the Iran Hostage Crisis, which saw 52 American diplomats and citizens held hostage for 444 days.

Amidst the juxtaposition of growth and decline, a television show was aired in 1983 with the purpose of teaching its audience, and unintentionally ignited the flame of ASMR. A military man turned painter, Bob Ross enlisted at the age of 18 and rose to the rank of Master Sergeant throughout his time serving in the United States Air Force. However, he decided to leave in 1981 when he realised he could earn more from his artwork than the military. Ross studied painting from the German artist, Bill Alexander; whilst working part-time in an Alaskan bar, Ross discovered Alexander hosting the show, *The Magic of Oil Painting*, and made contact with him. Ross absorbed the nuances of the paint palette like a sponge in water, adopting the 'wet on wet' technique, which is literal in its understanding – wet paint is applied on top of still wet paint.

'I started painting as a hobby when I was little. I didn't know I had any talent. I believe talent is just a pursued interest. Anybody can do what I do.'

-Bob Ross

Vowing he would never scream again, Bob Ross pursued a lucrative career in art that led him to create the television show, *The Joy of Painting*. *The Joy of Painting* was an instructional canvas painting show hosted by Bob Ross, and in each episode, he would walk you through how to paint a picture. Dubbed the 'Grandfather' of ASMR or the Master of ASMR by many members of the ASMR community, his shows would induce many peoples' ASMR, and watching his show, it is easy to see why. Bob Ross commands a soothing soft-spoken voice; his famous line, 'let's paint a happy little tree', is an instant trigger for some. Eroding the fourth wall, Bob Ross controlled the show with finesse, creating a feeling of safety amongst viewers and emphasising personal attention. Coupled with this are the various painting sounds, from brush strokes to the dabbing on the paint pallet – the show is an amalgamation of triggers.

How are we sure? Apart from sifting through all 403 episodes and achieving ASMR in the name of research, when people are asked about their early ASMR experiences, particularly in regards to media, *The Joy of Painting* is often cited as the answer. YouTube uploads of the show have received millions of views per episode; obviously, these are not all from ASMR viewers, but a significant portion is likely. Strikingly, before ASMR was a term, the show was noted for its relaxation. A 1990 article in the Orlando Sentinel commented: 'In part, the show's massive appeal can be attributed to Ross' personality. Like a Mr. Rogers with a palette, Ross whispers in hushed tones, painting in "a happy little tree" here and a "happy little cloud" there. For the frazzled viewer, his style is as

soothing as warm milk and cookies'. Despite the show being taken off the air in 1994, episodes continue to be watched today in order for people to get their virtual fix of 'warm milk and cookies'.

Turn of the Millennium

ASMR content originated, accidentally, with Bob Ross captivating his audiences through instruction and calm. Similar to the discovery of penicillin, accidents can bear the greatest fruit, and the same can be said for television and ASMR. At the turn of the millennium, the world was eagerly anticipating celebrations – or preparing for the impending global meltdown to be caused by the fictitious 'Y2K Bug'. Amongst the jovial and the doomsday preppers, a new reality series was making its way to the United Kingdom and the United States. The show was Big Brother.

The series takes its name from the character in George Orwell's 1984 in which Big Brother is the purported leader of the totalitarian state, wielding total power over its inhabitants. Premiering in the Netherlands, the series was created by John de Mol in 1997 and was embraced warmly by the Dutch. The show follows a number of 'housemates' who are isolated from the outside world in a purpose-built house fitted with multiple cameras. Each episode observes the contestants interacting with each other, performing various challenges and generally coping with their voluntary enclosure. Every week, a housemate is evicted via public vote until one winner emerges to claim the cash prize.

The relationship with ASMR is less obvious; in general, social drama and awkward tension are not as relaxing as nature landscapes. The triggering of a person's ASMR was a response to the contestants' nocturnal habits. Far from the carnal presumption you imagined, it actually ties in with the show's core theme of social interaction. Throughout all hours, housemates would turn to one another in hushed voices, recounting the day's events, or more likely, gossiping about another housemate. The microphones picked up these faint whispers and the rustling of the duvets, inducing relaxation.

2006

Two decades after the world learnt to paint 'a happy little tree', a new type of video emerged, the difference being that the videos were posted online. The leap from television to online independent creators is unsurprising and was to be expected. The cost of the technology required for making these amateur videos had decreased dramatically, making it affordable for households. Budding filmmakers were now able to dust off their old family cameras to not only film, but also make their projects available to the world. It was even possible to record video on your phone, putting a digital camera into the hands of mass consumers.

In 2006, there was a surge in traffic for online videos that witnessed the dawn of the funny cat videos and countless other internet cult classics, such as *'Charlie Bit My Finger'* – a personal favourite of mine. The ability to share your videos with anyone on the internet inspired generations to root out their old camera equipment and shoot . . . anything! I remember the first video that I ever uploaded to YouTube: myself and neighbourhood friends used an old camcorder to record our homage to George Romero's zombie legacy – whilst we were impressed with our feat, it was hardly a cinematic epic. The jarring camera angles and the dubious 'blood' acquired from a ketchup bottle slightly hindered the raw, gritty visual that we were trying to achieve. Amateur was the new craze; it was new and exciting. No one cared about the quality; everyone was finding their feet. However, what did matter was that the creative content was now harnessed by the historically passive participant in the entertainment scene – the viewer.

Alongside the freshly erected pillars of internet subculture was a new type of video that featured a product being unpackaged. These unboxing videos were predominantly tech-based and exploded that year, in part, due to the new video-game consoles that had been released by Sony, Microsoft and Nintendo. Eager gaming fans were chomping at the bit to get a glimpse of the latest offerings from their favourite companies, and quell their speculation and intrigue. The occasional unboxing would feature no talking, only the crinkling sounds of cardboard and plastic, gilded in glorious 240p (the highest resolution at the time). The creators themselves probably did not realise that they were indirectly filming what would later be known as an ASMR video, but people did find these videos relaxing. Videos such as these were the extent of ASMR content at the time; the tingling sensation still did not have a name, and it would be a few years before a video specifically designed for ASMR was uploaded – but the seeds were accidently sown nonetheless.

'I love making YouTube videos. I love talking to people I find interesting about stuff I find interesting and the internet is a great way to do that'

-John Green

It could be seen that any television show or YouTube video could have elements that trigger a person's ASMR; the barrier for entry is subjective after all. Regardless, these two shows, The Joy of

Painting and Big Brother, as well as early YouTube unboxing videos, deserve to be mentioned as they are forms of entertainment with segments that are clearly ASMR inducing, and they have a diverse viewer base – young and old, students and professionals – reflecting the spectrum of the ASMR phenomenon. The latter, YouTube, bears greater importance than the former; by reaching so many people, the portion who experience ASMR could expect to do so whenever they felt compelled by simply browsing online. In doing so, they raise their consciousness to the prospect that ASMR is not an arbitrary, once-off experience. The advent of the internet allowed people to use their experiences with these types of shows and ask questions. The anonymity afforded by the keyboard and mouse meant people were more confident to raise concerns about the tingly feeling inside their head and, in turn, found ASMR.

2007

The year had finally arrived when we witnessed the amplification of an underground movement. Lacking the aid of an official moniker to act as vanguard, people who felt ASMR were still unable to put a name to the tingling. The seeds had been sown, which sought an answer, the internet the roots from which it grew, and the discontent of ASMR experiencers the sunlight on which it fed.

A forum thread went live on *steadyhealth.com* on 19 October 2007 – the earliest remnants of the founding of ASMR. The author, *okaywhatever* (presumably a username, before all names were taken and the addition of 123 was forced), penned a statement titled: *'weird sensation feels good'*. The post explained the feeling that occurred when 'being read a story' or 'when a friend drew on the palm of [his] hand with markers'. The writer quickly indicates that the feeling is pleasurable: 'I love it'. The mysterious sensation percolates the same way as we understand ASMR to, which is in his 'head and all over [his] body'. The statement continues to paint a picture of what was felt by the author, the physical response could be considered unorthodox against the typical reaction to ASMR. The 'weird sensation' was so intense it caused his 'eyes to water'; the potency was increased if he 'itched' where he could feel the sensation, e.g. scalp.

The spark had ignited the fire; a somewhat extreme account of ASMR proved relatable in the comment section. Testimonies poured in that mirrored the sensation felt by *okaywhatever*. Continuing the apparent requirement of uninspired usernames, bean487 was the first to reply. The user noted a 'tingling in the scalp' that was caused by a slow speaking manner. He also sought out deliberate triggers opting for 'guided meditation tapes'. The post and the responses point towards the sensation being what we know as ASMR – it was even referred to as a 'head orgasm', courtesy of *bean487*.

The year 2007 marks the conception of the ASMR community, one random post on a website resonating with many more. The stone had been cast into the water, the leap had been taken, and the ripples that followed the writings of *okaywhatever* would connect a group of hundreds of thousands of people.

2008

If 2007 was the conception of the ASMR community, then 2008 represents the embryonic stage – morphing into something recognisable but still rough around the edges. The year is famous for the 'Great Recession', bringing economic downturn across the globe. Yet, its fame is not limited to the cyclical nature of boom and bust economics. Murmurings of the term AIHO, or attention induced head orgasm, began to circulate. The term was created by the user tingle on the same post on *steadyhealth.com* and proved attractive; the now defunct website *AIHO.org* launched later that year and prompted further discussion. The site appears to be the first dedicated to what we now recognise as ASMR, an important benchmark in the history of ASMR.

A Yahoo group formed in December that year (back when Yahoo was still a thing) who called themselves *The Society of Sensationalists*. Formed with the hopes of finding people who experience the same sensation, the results of their endeavours were similar to that of the thread on steadyhealth.com. Questions were being raised, but of answers there were none. AIHO threw the cat amongst the pigeons; it gave the movement new life, urging the search for answers forward. The search for answers would largely be in vain; a lack of consensus on what to call the sensation meant questions were not tethered to a specific term. The year 2008 was important in the understanding of ASMR; interest grew as did the community pursuing a resolution. However, it would be a couple of years until substantial progress was made.

2009

The year 2009 plays a pivotal role in the ASMR story; it is the year that the first ASMR video was published on YouTube. As you will discover in the second part of this book, the platforms the community adopts are key to the ASMR experience and the various media it uses. Without delving too far into the nitty-gritty now (I'll save that for later), the launch of the first ASMR video is monumental, especially as the term ASMR was not even accepted then. On 26 March 2009, the channel WhisperingLife uploaded

Whisper 1 hello; the description for the video opined: 'I know this might sound strange to some, but I love hearing people whisper so I thought I would make a whisper channel'.

In an interview with Dr Richard, WhisperingLife explained how she became inspired to take the first step into whispered content: 'I was watching a Big Brother video and reading through the comments. Someone had commented that they wished there was more whispering (I can't remember who it was). I then realised that I wasn't the only one watching these videos for the whispering. I then searched on YouTube for a channel dedicated to whispering but there wasn't one. That's when I decided I'd make my own. I had seen a few people express the same interest in whispering as I did, so I thought they might like to hear me whispering. I never knew so many people would like it! My channel grew pretty quickly. I did feel a bit odd at first, but I soon got into it (hence all the videos). Whispering to myself was also weirdly therapeutic for me. I didn't like listening to myself though.'

At the time of her posting, WhisperingLife may not have thought that a video of her plainly whispering would encourage swathes of people to follow suit, but I am glad she did. The space-age adage, 'one small step for man, one giant leap for man-kind', springs to mind; that one whisper video would go on to create a whole genre!

A New Dawn for ASMR

The world observed the birth of ASMR circa 2010, well, for the relatively small number of people it interested. Shakespeare once asked, 'What is in a name?'; for the ASMR community, its importance was implicitly clear. Forging a term that would universalise the definition of the sensation was not without its setbacks. Like Marco Polo, people were keen to make their mark and found the name that would identify their tingles first – alas, these noble thinkers adopted the keyboard and mouse over a galleass.

On 13 February, *The Unnamed Feeling* blog went live, founded by Andrew MacMuiris. Six days later, the founder released a statement commenting that AIHO had racy connotations and put forward that 'some do not associate it with sex'. Andrew, post denigration of AIHO, added to the melting pot of synonyms with AIOE or attention induced observant euphoria. AIOE appears to be inspired by the visual component of an ASMR experience and its link to the euphoric conclusion. To suggest that ASMR was suffering growing pains would be an understatement; confused about its own identity, different labels kept being attached to the sensation. It appeared that ASMR was drowning in a sea of acronyms, nomenclature that threatened to extinguish any intellectual interest in ASMR.

In ASMR's darkest hour, when all hope had seemed lost, the name was found. Jennifer Allen pioneered the name ASMR or autonomous sensory meridian response, emerging at some point during February 2010. In a 2012 interview with Vice, she explained how the name came about. She said that the terms such as autonomous, sensory and response are self-explanatory. Meridian replaced head orgasm in attempts to make it sound more authentic – 'try explaining why you want money to study head orgasms'.

In a 2016 interview with Dr Richard, Allen delved deeper into the motivation behind the term:

'People perceive the meaning of words differently, and a phrase that uses words tied to sexual or taboo activity, or words that have no immediate apparent connection to the topic tend to cause people to form opinions about the validity or intent of the subject at hand. I knew with something as difficult to describe and as sensitive for people to open up about as ASMR that we would need something that objectively and definitively named the sensation. Using a "clinical" word was the best option to improve how the burgeoning community would feel about using and telling others about the word. Critics like to call the term pseudoscientific, but I contend that in this climate of abject scepticism and

immediate gratification for knowledge, anything less formal or explicit would have failed to meet the needs in this very unique social circumstance. The name was what it had to be to help the community survive, and that was my mission.'

ASMR quickly consolidated its position as the accepted acronym – a name had finally been found.

Present Day

At the time of writing, ASMR has become the identifiable name adopted by the community and the general public for the tingly feeling. I briefly mentioned that finding an acceptable name would be important; its importance lies in the fact that it is a prerequisite for any further discovery to be made. The evidence is in the history. Four years were spent settling on a name, and the potential exploration lost in those years is tremendous – it is like an R&D team focusing all their resources on brainstorming a catchy name for a new product and putting no effort into the function of the product itself! Since 2010, appreciable strides have been taken: ASMR has its own dedicated day (9 April), scientists are beginning to delve into the sensation, and the ASMR community has built a bustling online platform.

The history of ASMR is as intriguing as the neurological reaction itself. A precise origin cannot be pinpointed, but even the history that we can record offers valuable insights into ASMR. It shows that the feeling has occurred longer than one may have originally thought, and demonstrates that it is not to be disregarded as a millennial fad – it is rich with notable characters, events and developments.

> *'The real voyage of discovery consists not in seeking new landscapes, but in having new eyes'*
>
> **-Marcel Proust**

PART 2

THE FELLOWSHIP OF THE TINGLES

BENJAMIN NICHOLLS

CHAPTER 4

Finding a Platform

Regardless of running an ASMR YouTube channel, as well as participating in the online community as a whole, the widespread discussion of ASMR in its mainstream, digital conception demonstrates that the internet has played a fundamental role in its growth and recognition. Periodically held in disrepute, it continues to expand, bleeding into every media platform possible: YouTube, podcasts, blogs, apps and news outlets to name just a few. It is the fervour of doting legions of ASMR fanatics, many of whom have spent years building up awareness and respect for the phenomenon, that has given people a voice – a common banner to rally behind.

Community is a familial word, one that reflects closeness and the bonds between clusters of individuals. A community works together to achieve a common goal, providing support for one another. Woven throughout the animal kingdom, the essence of community can be seen in humanity with our need to live close to other humans. Once in the form of tribes and now in the style of grand metropolises, it continues when scaling down to the humble fire ant, an insect who rids itself of individual concern and sacrifices itself to form a lifeboat, protecting its colony during floods.

Whether we realise it or not, we participate in innumerable communities and act differently in each one: your social circle, family and work all require unique interactions and approaches. Humans have an innate desire to fit in and to protect what is familiar. It is this idea of community that is the instrument that continues to drive the ASMR movement: social media groups, online videos, surveys and research papers all created by people yearning to understand ASMR's impact.

'Only a Life Lived for Others Is a Life Worthwhile'

-Albert Einstein

YouTube – The Patron Saint of ASMR

The purpose of this chapter is to explore the intricacies of ASMR platforms and their role in launching the response into popular media. It is impossible not to accredit significant praise to YouTube as the vehicle for ASMR's growth, both in terms of raising awareness and being at the forefront of administering 'tingles'.

Founded in 2005, YouTube was developed by Chad Hurley, Steven Chen and Jawed Karim. In fact, Karim was the first person to upload a video to the site, titled *'Me at the zoo'*. All former PayPal employees, the trio created a digital video streaming revolution that grew exponentially in a short period of time – all for the joy of sharing funny videos. July 2006 saw 100 million visitors to the site each day, and as of December 2016, YouTube received 22 billion visitors that month. The incredible traffic enjoyed by YouTube (or more accurately Google, who acquired the firm in October 2006) is stimulated by the popularity of burgeoning video types such as Vlogging (video-blogging) and Let's Plays (playthroughs of video games commentated by the player), genres that are centred around personalities. Essentially, YouTube is an ecosystem bringing together creative people and their eager audiences; equipped with only a camera, microphone and a decent broadband connection, anyone has the potential to communicate with millions of people around the world.

How is YouTube relevant to ASMR?

Mentioned throughout the book is the reference to 'ASMR media', the online content created with the purpose of triggering ASMR in the listener. YouTube is the apex distributer of ASMR videos; simply type ASMR into the YouTube search bar and you will be greeted by thousands upon thousands of diverse, occasionally bizarre, ASMR-related content. The sophisticated 'tags' on videos enable viewers to find specific trigger videos, but these videos are also recommended when simple phrases such as 'videos for sleep' or 'calming sounds' are searched.

The evolution of ASMR as a YouTube subculture has occurred gradually. Discussed in the previous chapter, the first ASMR video is believed to have been uploaded by WhisperingLife, titled *Whisper 1 hello*, on 26 March 2009 – a year before Jennifer Allen and her coining of 'ASMR' provided a unifying term. The channel may no longer be active, but its impact continues to this day as the initial spark that ignited the flame. However, the ignition was slow burning, and ASMR videos lay relatively dormant the following year. It began to snowball, gaining rapid momentum around 2011 on YouTube. Unified under one term, people in the community posted and viewed a growing number of ASMR videos. The channels that emerged around this time were relatively few; however, as it has blossomed, more and more people have tried their hand at creating relaxing content. In this sense, the creation of the term ASMR may have been a game changer; providing a unifying term lends itself to the successful searching and posting of content.

The ASMR community on YouTube have endured a turbulent rise (the controversial aspects of which are discussed later), as unlike vlogging or commentating over video games, ASMR isn't widely understood. People stumbling across an ASMR video randomly are unlikely to have a predicating knowledge about the type of video they are about to watch. You might suppose that this ignorance would preclude it from success; yet, in my experience, it is the resulting curiosity that has led to its triumph. Not only curiosity, the immediate effective relaxation may make folk immune to the logic of their experience and, hence, susceptible to the allure of ASMR.

Writing from personal experience, I came across ASMR completely by accident. Browsing YouTube, I saw that a channel that I subscribed to, TheBitBlock, had posted a new video. The channel uploaded typically video game-related content such as news and gameplay, although the title of this upload began with 'ASMR'. Clicking on it, intrigued, the video opened with the familiar host whispering and slowly working his way through an art book. I was transfixed. It was bizarre, but also incredibly relaxing and I didn't want to stop. A few minutes in, I began to feel a relaxing tingling sensation emanating from the top of my head, trickling through to the nape of my neck. Each page turn, every minutiae detail uttered in the hushed tone mystified and relaxed me. The feeling was faintly recognisable, having only experienced it in sporadic intervals in my past. My gaze wandered to the list of suggested videos alongside the current video playing – all ASMR. To avoid being overly hyperbolic, I won't refer to the experience as an epiphany, but it was a sort of a lightbulb moment.

From that video, I began my odyssey into the world of YouTube ASMR, watching a myriad of creators manipulating random objects for auditory delight. The interest bordered on obsession; I remember each morning before school sitting on my bed with my earphones plugged in, listening intently to new videos and dozing off again – not particularly helpful when you're not a morning person. To this day, I continue to use ASMR videos in the evenings to try and curtail my night-owl tendencies. Anyone you talk to has their own unique relationship with ASMR and how they stumbled upon the community. What I find so fortunate about my own is that it all occurred by chance – one curious click.

In a broad sense, YouTube has been a lifeline for ASMR. It has afforded a small community the tools to experiment with their identity, and to try and wrangle with the direction it should be taken in. We have already covered the general history of ASMR, but YouTube is a significant epoch in that timeline. The prevalence of ASMR content on non-ASMR channels demonstrates the pop-cultural impact that it has made in less than a decade. Cara Delevigne conducting an ASMR whispered interview for the W Magazine YouTube channel is one of countless examples showing that the ASMR community extends beyond the exclusivity of experiencing the sensory response. Impressive as it is, ASMR is still very much in its infancy. The largest ASMR YouTuber, GentleWhispering, has just surpassed one million subscribers – an impressive feat for any channel, although it reveals the community's market share is paltry compared to YouTube as a whole.

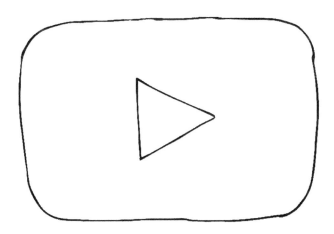

. . . But What Is An ASMR Video?

Prior to this section, I have done my best to illustrate a general sense of what an ASMR video consists of without delving into too much detail and, thus, deviating from the statement. Truth be told, concocting an accurate generalised perception of an ASMR video is difficult; the goalposts are completely fluid in the ASMR community, meaning that there is little to define a typical ASMR video. It might seem arbitrary to suggest that anything could be construed as ASMR, but the reasons being are likely due to the infancy of the community. Thus, as it grows so do the triggers, but more likely is the subjectivity of the response, and so any conversation regarding its validity as relaxing or stimulating is rendered moot.

Contrary to the ad infinitum I mentioned, the reality is that there exists a rough consensus regarding the distinct categories that ASMR videos fall into:

Trigger Videos:

Talked about in previous chapters, 'triggers' are certain aural or visual stimuli that literally trigger the euphoric sensation in your scalp. I have opted to promote trigger videos first as they are quintessentially the nucleus of ASMR – they exist in all other ASMR videos. The utilisation of specific sounds to induce a relaxing atmosphere is used in every type of ASMR video. The difference with dedicated trigger videos is just that – the video is dedicated to a solitary or a selection of triggers, instead of the trigger being incorporated into an ulterior theme. Often trigger assortments are favoured over the monotony of one sound, and the duration of each can range from a couple of minutes to 10 minutes or longer. The assortments can also be a random pick 'n' mix or a common collection, e.g. an assortment of mouth sounds could include lip smacking, tongue clicking and inaudible whispering.

At face value, this type of content may seem mundane; even the idea of someone sitting in front of a camera, brushing a microphone for 60 minutes can seem risible. Attempting to convince you otherwise could be futile. Perhaps, seeing it for oneself is the simplest solution – but given the relative absurdity of ASMR, if I didn't attempt to decipher its curiosity and told you to just look it up instead, this would make an already short book even smaller. YouTubers who decide to make trigger compilations often work away from the boring premise, wanting to inject life into a drab starting point.

A technique known as layering is one of the ways that content creators get inventive; the process involves playing multiple soundtracks over one another to create a symphony of harmonious, lazed sounds. A particular use of layering that I am fond of is the natural convergence of sounds in different environments. Coffee shops and libraries are designed as an escape from the hustle and bustle of everyday life, and it is as if the furnishings are conscious of that fact – the turning of pages, the sipping of a hot beverage against the backdrop of hushed chatter works seamlessly to put me at ease – I'm not the only one, right?

Various colours on the spectrum are also used at times. Titled *'follow the light'*, the concept is rather literal and the viewer is invited to trace the paths carved by the illuminations – against a dark backdrop the visuals are quite compelling. Constant experimentation, typical of a fledgling, bohemian practice, has led to discoveries; for example, February 2013 bore witness to a new sound trigger, phonetically referred to as 'sk', in Heather Feather ASMR's *Ten Triggers to Make You Tingle*. Presumably not something you hear every day, out of context, it is like voluntarily watching someone hiss at you for a good 20 minutes. Perhaps due to eccentricity or variability, trigger videos are profoundly popular, with a range garnering millions of views a piece.

Unearthing the reason why these types of videos are favoured above the rest is difficult to ascertain; it is probable that videos focused on trigger sounds are typically lengthy in duration (30–60 minutes on average), meaning people can watch, unwind and drift off without the need to check their phone repeatedly to change the video. They also serve as perfect introductory videos. The testimonies of many viewers talk about how alien ASMR is at first glance; so, watching someone tap a box or scratch their carpet can help newbies explore and develop their personal portfolio of preferred sounds.

'The Empty Vessel Makes the Loudest Sound'

-William Shakespeare

Let's Plays:

Let's plays are serious business on YouTube, earning the most successful personalities millions of subscribers, views and most tangibly, dollars. In their simplest form, a let's play consists of the video-maker playing through a video game (with the footage of both player and game displayed) whilst commentating on their progress. To the uninitiated, watching someone else play a game may be mindboggling and wonder why the viewer isn't playing the game for themselves. The obvious rebuttal is to apply the same logic to sport, and wonder why people tune in to watch football week in and week out. These types of videos have given rise to internet superstars such as PewDiePie, currently the #1 subscribed channel on YouTube with 50+ million subscribers, and the eSports genre as a whole. Fans are fanatical about their favourite let's players and eSports teams, and as a result, it has developed into an incredibly lucrative market (rough figures from the Wall Street Journal suggest PewDiePie, real name Felix Arvid Ulf Kjellberg, earned $7.4 million in 2014). The market is so attractive, in June 2011, it spawned YouTube rival, Twitch.tv, a site dedicated to livestreaming let's plays and other content.

Given the immense backing by digital consumers, ASMR YouTubers have modified the genre to be a tad more user friendly for their typically reposed audience; anyone familiar with the virtual play-through should find that unsurprising. Let's plays tend to be rather . . . colourful in tone, especially playing through horror titles (the entertainment value of watching someone leap in fear whilst playing a scary game is incredibly satisfying).

I certainly enjoy the ASMR version of let's play; video games as a whole is the area to which my content is largely tailored to, forming a significant chunk of my persona in the community (so much so it is in my channel's name: The ASMR Gamer). Certainly, video games were the impetus for me launching my own channel; it is a hobby rich with entertainment, offering a cornucopia of video ideas for my business. Not to delve too deeply into the dark basements of 'nerdom', but there are scores of different video-game types, from exploring vast lush environments in role-playing games (RPGs) to the pixelated platforming of a fat Italian plumber. Assuming the gameplay is not jarring and the player can maintain a calm voice, any game can plausibly be played and enjoyed in an ASMR setting.

Time to talk about a specific title that has flourished within this subset of content in both the ASMR sphere and the normally voiced; fear not, if you're not a video-game aficionado (you should be), I won't going into in-depth specifics about the game. The name of this curious game is perhaps familiar even to those who have never picked up a controller; the cubic universe and boundless crafting possibilities have cemented *Minecraft* in modern culture. For the uninitiated, *Minecraft* is a sandbox (open world) game that encourages players to gather resources, fend off monsters and construct buildings from textured blocks. Officially launched in 2011, *Minecraft* has launched on practically every modern gaming device – from PC to iPhone – selling 122 million copies as of February 2017.

Interest in the game isn't exclusive to the creative freedom it offers players. Additionally, it enables them to participate in an atmosphere of calm; gamers progress at their own pace, serenaded by a tranquil soundtrack, fabricating the illusion of time passing faster than you realise – what felt like minutes were instead multiple hours as players immerse themselves in virtual projects. The amalgam of blissful components that make up Minecraft reflects how it became such a hit for those seeking head tingles – the game was a natural fit. ASMR channels, such as theASMRnerd, run series such as *Pixel Paradise* or *Wandering in Skyrim*, which involve a whispered exploration throughout various environments and scenarios. The artistic nature of the games allows viewers to suspend reality and focus on the whispers, providing a true relaxation escape.

In a nutshell, let's plays have proven a hit among the ASMR community, giving rise to channels such as my own and many more. The calm guidance echoes that of guided meditation, allowing the viewer to drift off whilst they are taken on an adventure – but not too adventurous!

> 'With patience, perseverance and consistency, hopefully the ASMR let's play genre will be its own monster to be reckoned with one day . . . albeit a calm, softly spoken monster'
>
> **-Ephemeral Rift**

The Romance of Role Plays:

If you have read/watched anything to do with ASMR before reading this book, the likelihood is that you have come across the concept of role playing; the Oxford English dictionary defines it as '[to] act out or perform the part of a person or character', otherwise known as acting. The difference is subtle as role playing tends not to be in front of an audience per se; instead, it is for the entertainment of the performers themselves. Role playing tends to reside in the realms of fantasy; live action role playing (LARPing) is a common form involving folk donning costumes of knights, wizards and elves, depending on the source material. I am sure the less socially prude of my readers will be aware of the lewder role playing . . . the less said about that the better; writing about head orgasms is awkward enough without discussing French maids or bunny rabbits!

An ASMR role play is a comparable beast in and of itself. Rather than dressing in elaborate costumes and immersing oneself in alternate realities, the characters that are often selected are real-world occupants – hairdressers, tailors and doctors are all vacancies that have been filled in the ASMR employment centre. Video makers adopt these professions with all the trimmings; the content consists entirely of how that service is conducted: a hairdressing role play will see someone consult, wash and trim your hair; a tailor will grab a tape measure, size you up, discuss fabrics and more; the doctor/medical role plays usually focus on a consultation or exam, such as a cranial nerve exam.

Determining why these 'characters' are chosen is relatively easy when you examine the context of the performances; the correlation between them all is their emphasis on close, intimate, personal attention. Mentioned in part one, before the internet, people experienced ASMR through the prism of everyday, pretty mundane activities, and those who experienced the sensation must have found it relaxing as it has been adopted into ASMR role plays.

ASMR, as always, leaves its own unique stamp on all it touches. Touched upon further in the next chapter, it wouldn't be surprising if you found all of this rather strange, weird or just completely bizarre – to an extent I can sympathise; I myself have filmed an array of quirky role plays. Venturing away from the doctor's office, I have adopted the roles of a zombie apocalypse survivor, a student at Hogwarts, and James Bond himself! But I am merely a novice; I recommend you explore the creative talents of Heather Feather, Tony Bomboni, and Ephemeral Rift. Ephemeral Rift is particularly enthralling with the quirky casts of characters and story arcs he has developed. Role plays offer a visceral outlet for creativity, building a universe that you share with your audience in a relaxingly meaningful manner.

Experimentation and ASMR are inextricably linked; the community relishes in exploration, the yearning for new ways to tingle is effervescent. Researching characters, scripting storylines and acquiring props is all part of the process. Ask any ASMR creator and they will all say that role plays provide artistic freedom; it is this freedom to push the boundaries that has proven popular among audiences.

I implore you to put this book down and try to find the strangest role play out there; if you come across clowns or puppets . . . you're not thinking weird enough

Three-Dimensional Audio:

3D movies, 3D televisions and 3D printers – we have become obsessed with the creative oil fields that the third dimension allows us to rig into. The use of 3D in visual entertainment has previously been reserved for visual effects: the monster leering out of the screen to grab you, the post-explosion shrapnel flying into the theatre ala Michael Bay, or the intense immersion through a seemingly tangible fantasy world as in James Cameron's *Avatar*. It appears that the audiophiles are now receiving their fair share of 3D wonderment with the introduction of 3D audio. 3D sound presents an artificial listening experience in concert to how you hear in life. Rejecting mono (one direction) and enhancing stereo (multiple directions) audio, 3D microphones capture up to 360° of sound to offer a truly immersive auditory experience not seen since surround sound.

    The implementation of 3D in entertainment has been overwhelmingly lacklustre, being used as a commercial ploy rather than intensifying the storytelling; therefore, it is seen by many as gimmicky. The deteriorating palate for 3D, in tandem with the expense associated with the technology, means it is a niche market, and far more so for 3D audio. The ASMR community is a big proponent and investor of the 3D audio landscape. Voracious creators are constantly looking for an edge, the latest tool to offer their viewers incontestable immersion; 3D audio is used by these creators in all types of videos to stimulate the ears and keep them engaged. Through the use of headphones, it is amazing the depth of audio that can be achieved, as the creator moves around, so too does the sound being relayed to you.

Audio quality is obviously paramount to the ASMR experience, putting pressure on the creator to pick the Goldilocks microphone, the device that is just right. Decisions vary between audio that is of a more professional quality, crisp and clear, or more rustic, low-fidelity (lo-fi) audio that has a lot of white noise. The ASMR community's interest in 3D audio has introduced a new factor to consider when assembling your kit. Microphones with 3D audio capabilities tacked on already exist on the market, but there are new microphones being invented purposefully for 3D. The firm 3DIO produce distinct 3D microphones, featuring ears as the receptors, to lead the market in ASMR and VR audio capture. The *Free Space Binaural Microphone*, designed with two ears, is a popular choice on the ASMR circuit that when used incites the sensation of being directly spoken into your ear. Yet, 3D microphones aren't the norm due to their expense; the microphone I just mentioned sets you back $499, with the most expensive *Omni Pro Binaural Microphone*, with a discombobulating amount of ears, punishing your wallet by $5499.

Now, 3D microphones aren't the status quo and, hence, the infrequency of 3D ASMR videos. Whispering binaurally from ear to ear is still more popular than full 3D audio, but the capabilities of the technology are vast. I can imagine that as the tech becomes cheaper, putting it into the hands of more creators, the quality of role plays, trigger videos, etc. will rocket – after all, who doesn't enjoy whispers straight into their ear canal?

Mukbang:

South Korea. Arguably the technological capital of the world, renowned for its rich culture, innovations (the first MP3 player originated from S. Korea), and a rather unfortunate noisy northern neighbour. Aside from glorious internet speeds, South Koreans also have an interest in cuisine, the basis for mukbang. To those not fluent in Korean, mukbang roughly translates into 'eating broadcast'; rather self-explanatory, participants will stream themselves eating a range of meals whilst interacting with their audience – mukbang takes the pleasure of eating to a new level.

The uniqueness of mukbang led to it quickly spreading across the globe. Lambasted by some as gross and as oddly satisfying by others, it was readily absorbed into the ASMR spectrum. As social creatures, mealtimes have historically been an opportunity to gather, converse and enjoy, and this is no different today; visiting a restaurant is valued by all. Whether it is an informal, quick bite to eat at your local McDonald's or an opulent fine dining evening at a Michelin star restaurant, the basic function is the same: to come together and eat. Yet, does that make mukbang any less odd? Arguably, I believe it does; mukbang is a digitised restaurant experience (bar the brick & mortar and the waiting staff) with predominantly only one person actually eating any food. The conversation, the reactions to the food, and the accompanied chewing can induce a relaxing vibe, perhaps even a comfort. Thus, ASMR mukbang was born, quickly becoming one of my more preferable video types to turn to – ingredients for a good night's rest: yourself, a pillow, and a video of someone gorging on tasty delicacies!

WARNING: Potential nightmare for sufferers of misophonia . . . moreover, it can leave you feeling incredibly hungry – bring snacks.

ASMR Fatigue

A peculiar discovery was detected amidst the abundance of ASMR content ripe to be binged, and that is the dilution of the response, even complete desensitisation, following prolonged sessions. Typically experienced through excessive use of narcotics, overstimulating receptors in our body causes our body to be less receptive, meaning we need to either up the dosage or potency, or steer clear to allow the body time to recover. Comparably, reports from frequent ASMR viewers are claiming that whilst they are still able to use ASMR auspiciously for sleep, they have noticed a decline in actual ASMR experiences; the triggers that were once a reliable source are no longer fulfilling. ASMR is understood to be a pleasurable experience, and as such, it appears to respond in the same way as pleasure-inducing vices, providing on-demand euphoria. It manipulates the body's reward system, circumventing required effort, such as exercise for a 'runners high', for instant gratification. Mimicking the traits of other neurological chemicals, the reality of ASMR fatigue acts as ancillary proof that ASMR is real.

The damaging effect that ASMR fatigue has is foreseeably minimal: it doesn't encourage the use of harder relaxation techniques (whatever they are), and the sensation is said to return once given a reasonable berth for a while. I myself have coped with the absence of tingles for a number of months, and I am still able to enjoy a swift transition to sleep with my favourite triggers. My line of work makes it rather difficult to avoid ASMR for stretches of time, and there are brief pockets of faint tingles but not the effervescent euphoria I experienced in the early days. From personal experience, I wouldn't worry about exhausting your

ASMR capacity – eight hours' sleep surpasses the fleetingness of tingles in the grand scheme of things.

'Artists'

Beethoven to Banksy, artists have endowed the world with exquisite music, art and literacy, each a poignant reflection interpreting the state of society or personal philosophy. Art is inherently subjective, including the definition of an artist, meaning who can credibly identify as one remains a moot point. The only generality is the production of something, tangible or intangible. Debates flare up questioning the legitimacy of cinema as an art form, or more controversially, video games. Both harbour traditional art prerequisites: a story, visuals and a musical score, with the only discernible difference being how the art is communicated. It is the ambivalence of art that underscores this section, not precise discussion – I couldn't distinguish the work of Holbein from Da Vinci if I wanted to (art has never been my strong suit – self-portraits in my high-school art class rarely evolved from stick figures).

Online content creators, as they grow, attain a pseudo-celebrity status, reaping greater recognition and significant clout in their respective fields and beyond. This also applies to the smaller world of ASMR; the ASMR creators with the larger followings carry palpable influence, becoming unofficial spokespeople, shaping the public perception of ASMR through interviews, etc. Does this make them artists? Is digital video, specifically the whispering kind, a new form of artistry, on par with respected creative crafts? It poses an interesting question, one that is pertinent to ASMR culture; 'artist' is popularly used to refer to ASMR creators, both by themselves and their audience – playfully coined 'ASMRtist', it clearly denotes the content that they produce.

Is it warranted? Innocently titular as it may be, and even though I have referred to myself and others as one in the past, it is difficult to shake the air of pomposity it musters. Labelling oneself as an artist immediately assumes you are culturally impactful, and at the very least, creating something of beauty or inspiration. Still a fledgling community, on one hand, it could be seen that such self-proclamation can incite more criticism, rather than conveying the benefits that it produces. Arrogance is the wrong way to increase positive exposure and reputation – it can feel smug. On the other hand, art is an emotionally personal outlet; just because an artist isn't deemed popular doesn't negate their works – after all, beauty is in the eye of the beholder.

I am not dismissing the term or vilifying the ASMRtists (including myself) outright. Inciting head tingles requires both technical and imaginative wherewithal. The video production side alone is a drawn-out, laborious affair for those who aren't camera savvy. Filming a plain, purely whispered video still requires the right camera and lens for the right look. Then, you need to pair it with a suitable microphone (of which there is strong diversity: shotgun mics, lavaliers, binaural . . .). Throw in some props and a green screen, then the production becomes doubly complex to fulfil a vision.

Are the works of ASMRtists bona fide art? I verge on the no; I am not convinced that it is, and view it more as straightforward entertainment (although I am sure that there are others who believe entertainment is a form of art). I should stress that I also don't take umbrage with people identifying and using the term ASMRtist. Creativity is involved and it does genuinely change the lives of many people, and for that I am proud to associate myself with a genuine, inclusive community. This isn't an attack on the ASMR community (the book in your hands is a labour of love to said group). I just find it a peculiar moniker to adopt, especially the potential connotations that follow.

If nothing else, ASMRtist equips me with another name to use instead of recycling content creator or producer!

'No great artist ever sees things as they really are. If he did, he would cease to be an artist'

-Oscar Wilde

The Heart of the Community

The ASMR community is predominantly defined through YouTube, Facebook groups, and Reddit; identity, growth and evolution, the internet essentially brought together likeminded people trying to figure out the alien scalp sensation they enjoy. There is no denying that ASMR remains a minutiae spec on the digital landscape; compared to passions not dissimilar to ASMR, such as yoga and meditation, they far outweigh ASMR in both active participants and understanding. Despite inferior numbers, the community is still fiercely loyal and passionate, equal to any community.

Posting online, you always take a personal risk, opening yourself up for criticism and taunting. The prevalence of 'trolls' plagues any internet domain. Hurling abuse from the sanctity of their keyboards, it can be seriously demotivating, crushing the creativity of some. The presence of ASMR online is not immune to invective thought, nor should it be. Scroll down and read the comments on any ASMR-related piece of content and you will find a derogatory comment. I don't have to look far on one of my own videos to see someone comment: 'this is messed up sh*t' or 'this is perverted'. Although, I never quite understand how they got to that part of YouTube without some deliberate browsing.

Writing the notes for this segment, I didn't want denigration to eclipse the message; it serves to exhibit the collective might that this small group has. As both viewer and creator, I have witnessed and experienced the passion that is seemingly ubiquitous in the community. Unlike other forms of entertainment that can spark internal, divisive tribalism, most involved with ASMR seem positive, wanting others to relax, unwind and succeed. Scroll down again to the comment section of an ASMRtist; notice the multitude of positive comments, supporting the creator, expressing personal testimonies regarding their life pivoting for the better after discovering ASMR. Not only that, trolls are actively targeted, reducing their comments to petulance.

At its heart, ASMR is designed to allow people to feel good; nasty competition has no place – although it does exist. On the surface, there is an undeniable harmony between viewer and ASMRtist, stemming from all creators being fanatics themselves. Fervour has been vital to get ASMR to where it is today. With something so seemingly taboo, or at least it used to be, any flicker of interest in the early days could have easily been snuffed out without the support network that ASMR has cultivated.

Throughout the years, progress has been sedated, happily trundling along waiting for the next discovery, albeit until YouTube took ASMR off of the back foot and catalysed intrigue and research. It is said a community is the sum of all its parts, meaning like any successful political party, the health of ASMR cannot rely on a single solitary platform (i.e. YouTube). In lieu of extensive scientific research, there are a substantial number of media channels that the ASMR community is pursuing to push the boundaries, and increase understanding, credibility and new audiences.

Websites + Apps:

Type anything into Google and you are sure to find a website that is linked to that search: a cat playing piano? Done. Irrefutable proof for the existence of Atlantis? You bet! The same is true for ASMR. A variety of websites exist that centre on ASMR and all its nuances; a particular favourite of mine is one I mentioned previously, *ASMRUniversity.com*. A website curated by Dr Richards, *ASMRUniversity.com* serves as a concise database chronicling all things ASMR, and was an invaluable tool in researching this book.

It is also Dr Richard who generously helped fine tune this book via feedback on my initial drafts, adding invaluable insights!

Aside from information, alternatives to viewing ASMR videos are also available; iOS and android stores feature apps such as *TingleFM*, leading you straight to the ASMR content. I am of the persuasion that apps will be a strong vehicle for ASMR. I launched The ASMR Gamer app in early 2016 to an enthusiastic reception. The app provides direct access to my content that is available to download, alleviating the issues incurred from a lack of internet access, providing ASMR on the go. It also includes features such as my schedule, requests and general feedback; before too long, I imagine swathes of ASMRtists will venture into branded apps to provide a bespoke, convenient ASMR experience.

Literature

The written word is arguably mankind's most significant construction; it erects civilisations and cures disease through the ability to transmit a consistent code of text. Knowledge is king. To encourage debate, there needs to be information readily available to draw upon; in that regard, the ASMR community is succeeding. Scientific papers, as mentioned, are woefully scarce, as are books, with the only notable published book being the *Idiot's Guides: ASMR* by Julie Young and Ilse Blansert. Fortunately, online news articles are in abundance; from VICE to BBC News, news coverage about ASMR interests the whole journalistic spectrum. The majority of articles scratch the surface of ASMR, opting to focus on the quirkiness and inviting popular ASMRtists to contribute. ASMR remains a buzzword, boding well for the prospect of future investigation.

Film

Documenting phenomena on film is an opportunity to explore topics in a visceral manner, communicating expressions and emotions that are perhaps more obtuse in literary form. Online you can find a couple of independent documentaries that focus on the ASMRtists that populate the community. One such video, titled *ASMR [Road Trip]*, produced by the channel True Binaural & ASMR, tours the UK interviewing various creators to learn about their experiences with the world of ASMR. A more recent two-part documentary, produced by Rooster Teeth, features the typical interviews of prominent ASMRtists, but also ventures to India to visit the 'Cosmic Barber of Pushkar', famed for the 'World's Greatest Head Massage'. The documentaries broadcast the essence of ASMR to a larger, diverse group, rather than the echo chamber that permeates the ASMR community. Unfortunately, although successful Kickstarter projects exist for in-depth documentaries, their production has gone eerily quiet the past few years. For example, Braingasm and Tingly Sensation: The ASMR Story raised $15,330 CAD and $11,202 USD, respectively, yet no public word has been issued on their sites regarding progress.

The films are not all documentaries; an indie film titled Murmurs, a more cinematic, fictional depiction of ASMR, is in the works. The plot centres around 'a reclusive ASMR superstar invit[ing] an online date to her studio. A paranoid romance with tingles.' It is exciting to see ASMR incorporated into storytelling as a subtle device for character arcs. According to an update post on their indiegogo page, the film was finished on 9 August 2017, and they are in the process of distributing to film festivals prior to online release.

The Convention of Conventions

The world is a small place; the advent of the internet connected people globally without having to pop in a car, train or aeroplane. Friendships, even romantic relationships, have sprung forth from the interconnected World Wide Web. Groups and communities exist for every passion and hobby out there; so, whatever your escape from the stresses of the world is, you can find others just like you. Instant messaging and video chat have enabled bonds of friendship to form absent of physical proximity; what they lack in face-to-face encounters, they make up for with an abundance of shared passion. It is these passions, and a desire to come together to celebrate, that have influenced the huge rise in conventions throughout the world. Comic-Con, VidCon, MineCon, BlizzCon, and Summer in the City are just a small fragment of conventions that form a mosaic of niche-fuelled extravaganzas, with hundreds of thousands swarming to their dedicated conventions to socialise, peruse merchandise and immerse themselves in their hobbies – all facilitated by the internet.

The ASMR community, for all its messages of connectivity and closeness, is just beginning to take baby steps towards the monoliths that are dedicated conventions. It isn't an issue of numbers; the ASMR community grows by the droves every day. The issue lies with the nature of the beast (and organisation). Hangouts do occur; whether it is an ASMRtist meeting a handful of their fans or fellow creators getting together, there is an appetite to meet up with the friends made on this journey. An attempt was made to bring together the ASMR fanatics of the world with the ASMR World Tour, which hoped to kick-off on the North American East Coast in 2014. The project was set to bring together creators and viewers via a roaming bus tour from Toronto to New York, opting for a rolling hop-on/hop-off strategy. Unfortunately, the ambitious project fizzled out due to organisational dilemmas involved with concerting a tour of intercontinental scope. Since then, there has been no concentrated effort to organise a largescale gathering.

Surely as the community continues to grow inordinately, efforts will be reprised, learning from the lessons of trying to achieve too much and focus small, e.g. one city, then grow it from there. I imagine an ASMR-Con would be rather enjoyable: traversing the stalls; attending panels debating topical pieces; and pleasantly hearing a concerto of hushed tones, rather than the melee of other Cons. What a platform that would be!

I have made numerous friends through my involvement within the community, spanning the globe: French, Italian, German, American, Israeli, Malaysian, Singaporean, Korean, Japanese and Australian. I am not unique in this regard. ASMRtists and viewers all create their own network of ASMR friends through the social media groups they're involved with, or even the conversations struck in the comment section of a video. It would be incredible to have the opportunity for the world's ASMR community to meet up at a specialised convention – all we need is an ASMR fan with an abundance of disposable income to orchestrate it!

One day, ASMR-Con will happen.

Togetherness

Attempting to write about a community, with its own culture, practices and traditions, can be a daunting prospect. I found collating all the areas ASMR has influenced rather difficult, being such a young and almost abstract physiological sensation. Conducting research, I had the pleasure of speaking to Emma of WhispersRed ASMR, a channel with 70+ million views. Emma hosted what might be considered the world's first live, in person, en masse ASMR performance at The Courtyard Theatre, London, earlier in 2017. We spoke about the representation of ASMR:

'Awareness of ASMR in the UK seems to be growing steadily. There are so many ASMR content creators over here and, indeed, the first whisper video ever made was by an English YouTuber. ASMR content and triggers have also been featured in art installations around the country for a few years now. There is definitely a culture of open mindedness, adventure and spirituality over here, which opens the doors for anything deemed to be therapeutic for the soul. ASMR has so many facets and appeals to many communities.

When I think about how ASMR is presented in the UK, I can only comment from my own experience and say that at every given opportunity all I have ever done is talk about how wonderful it is. I am keen to explore the therapeutic aspect of the physical feeling itself and am hoping one day we will have a better insight into how it happens in our bodies. The videos themselves are very artistic at times as well as providing comfort and entertainment for so many around the world. I can only see positive in what we do in the ASMR community and can only show this when I explain it to others. It is very understandable how the ASMR videos and the feeling can be initially seen as something else, especially to those that don't experience the sensation. However, I believe that is more a reflection on our society and the way we advertise products, music and celebrities. I find that once I can explain how the ASMR sensation and the videos work, the majority of people are able to relate very quickly. Therapeutic treatments, both practical and spiritual, are nothing new at all. I believe ASMR is a new one to the list, that's all.'

Whether it is tapping in front of a camera then posting the video online; writing, filming and developing ASMR products; meeting up with the friends you have made throughout the community; even orchestrating a huge project such as Emma's, ASMR has certainly found a platform. In less than a decade, ASMR has created a market based upon wellbeing and connectivity, pushing the boundaries with each passing year with more people swelling the ranks. As the community's reach expands, more are exposed, leading to more having the eureka moment, with the dots connected between that strange feeling they never previously understood.

Finding a platform is at the heart of the ASMR story. In an ever-growing state (there are even ASMR spas popping up designed to trigger your ASMR), the possibilities for ASMR are vast. With great strides in technology, such as virtual reality, the ASMR experience and the community will only intensify (in a calm manner, of course).

CHAPTER 5

Growing Pains: A Storm of Scepticism

The elusive dark side: whether it is the Moon or Star Wars, everything has a dark side – including the world of ASMR. Throughout this account, I have attempted to convey a positive message regarding ASMR, and I strongly agree with that sentiment. Perhaps suggesting that ASMR has a dark side is a tad sinisterly hyperbolic; it isn't evil per se – it is hardly attempting world domination. However, as with anything new, it can be strange, harbouring criticism from those who don't really understand it, nor particularly want to. Criticism isn't just external; as something grows it can alter, morphing as it matures (cue another adolescent teen cliché). The world of ASMR is new, impressionable and with a great deal of understanding still lurking in the recesses of our mind. Through this transition from a private experience to a trendy topic of conversation, it has been criticised in various ways, namely weirdness, sexualisation, pseudo-science and becoming a sell-out. As the book draws to a close, I thought it would be appropriate to take a step back and try to analyse ASMR from the perspective of an ASMR novice and how they may approach each criticism.

'We do not fear the Unknown. We fear what we think we know about the Unknown'

-Teal Swan

Eerie Strangeness

If you had to describe the ASMR experience, you would be hard pushed not to include the words 'weird' or 'bizarre'; weird isn't bad, often it is the start of intellectual arousal. As we are inquisitive creatures, the unknown is a potent force and the allure is intoxicating, difficult to suppress. Yet, weirdness tends to skew public perception, with those unfamiliar trying to wrap their heads around the foreign concept. Unsurprisingly, weirdness finds itself the lens through which media outlets tend to communicate ASMR. For those savvy with the ASMR scene, you're probably desensitised and numb to the relative obscurity of ASMR and the videos made; but if you're not, and that is perhaps the majority of the internet, it can be a bizarre place, and you can be forgiven for scepticism as a result.

College Humor, an award-winning YouTube comedy sketch show, did a skit on ASMR, placing the lead in alarming situations whilst retaining a calm composure. The video opens with a woman narrating her makeup routine in a hushed whisper, just like any other ASMR video, right? Shortly after, a burglar enters and begins robbing her; again, no voices are raised. A policeman follows suit to apprehend the reposed burglar, the scene quickly unravelling into a low-decibel comical bloodbath. It is an amusing skit, satirising some outsiders' interpretation of the varied role plays that populate YouTube. As you know, ASMR can be triggered by all sorts of activities, meaning it is understandable that people can find it rather odd when a kidnapping or a Pinocchio-style puppet role playing (yes, they exist) gets millions of views.

Even credible news sites, such as the BBC, have commented on ASMR, acknowledging that there might be something to it, but that it is rather weird. In the article *ASMR: What's Going On Inside My Brain*, author Nick Higham wrote, 'there's still plenty we do not know about ASMR . . . but we do know that the number of ASMR videos just keep on growing . . . however weird they may seem'.

There is no serious damage nor controversy resulting from the perceived weirdness of ASMR. I suppose there is a slight chance it precludes genuine journalistic inquiry when editors get caught up in the costumes and camera stroking (a trigger I forgot to mention).

After all, it will garner higher clicks than an article centred on neurology. It does make explaining ASMR rather challenging; a common question I am asked is: 'How do you explain what you do (ASMR) to friends and family?'; it is a reasonable question given that ignorant people pillory ASMRtists online, one might wonder how close ones would react. Truth be told, I only told friends and family about my whispering exploits once my channel gained traction. They all understood YouTube, but confusion arose when I continued to explain what it is I do and the tingling sensation I seek. I didn't blame them for finding my use of saliva as an instrument off-putting, and it was difficult to argue in favour of a 30-minute video featuring someone folding bath towels as the norm.

Although my personal relationship with ASMR has been favourable, with an understanding and supportive network of family and friends – let's be honest, if they weren't it would be difficult to ask them to be quiet when I am trying to film, and even then, I have to edit out the odd bleating from housemates – for some, telling others about ASMR isn't always met with a jubilant reception. For many, there is a real possibility of sounding like a 'weirdo', or there explanations of their experiences being misconstrued as a sexual fetish. It is a shame that many keep their involvement in the community a secret; it demonstrates the effect that doing something a little different, putting your head above the parapet, can have. ASMR is an incredible environment to participate in; there should be no expectation of bullying for talking about a fascinating bodily reaction. With further embedment of ASMR in the media and the continuing discussion by the community, the ASMR experience will hopefully become somewhat normalised.

Basked in randomness, a niggling question I still ponder is: Why is ASMR so alien, if its roots lie in anthropology?

If you scratch away the paraphernalia of ASMR, looking purely at the sensation and not at the fictitiously superfluous role-play scenarios that can mar perception, it is no different to goosebumps or pins and needles. Purely biological responses to external stimuli . . . nothing E.T. about that. Does that mean we, the community, have made it weird? If so, does it matter? It is conceivable to assume that the physiological reaction wouldn't sustain interest. Initially it would, of course, yet it would die a swift death in mainstream media due to the sluggish research and developments that are presently occurring. Therefore, it is how it has been adopted – infused with creativity and unpredictability, it stays on the tip of the internet's tongue; to anthropomorphise the adjective further, weirdness has benefited the ASMR community in many ways.

To my mind, it would be reasonable to assume that ASMR will become normalised, even vindicated of its strangeness, in the years to come. It is rapidly becoming commonplace as a topic of debate within the majority of media, meaning it should trickle down into everyday life. Reflecting on recent gatherings with friends, I would be asked about how the channel was going with real interest, and what lay in store for the community as a whole, in stark contrast to the jibes and 'witty' comments that would previously have been made. Although some of my friends, from time to time, continue to refer to me as a porn-star, drawing a false equivalency between the two types of euphoria, not helped by the term 'head orgasm'.

ASMR might exhibit qualities deemed weird, strange, incomprehensible, outlandish, freakish and zany, but that is nothing to be ashamed of, for those characteristics keep it salient and allow the community to flourish and to make it stand out.

$ex $ells

The world, as a whole, is a remarkably liberal place (give or take a handful of backwards, fundamentalist nations) compared to a century ago. If you teleported to the 19th century, abducted a typical Victorian Englishman, then dropped him in the middle of any Pride march today, he would be stunned at the civil liberties and acceptance we enjoy, and how we are better off because of it.

And whilst bigotry hasn't been eradicated, it is rightfully countered rather than continuing as the status quo. The keenest liberation is our relationship, or more accurately, our openness with sex; sex is no longer taboo. Awkwardness has dissipated and we are much happier discussing our sexual proclivities with others, the enlightenment being expedited through the adoption of sexually suggestive content by mass communications – just look at any perfume advert, YA novel or music video.

The old adage, sex sells, is as true now as it has ever been, even more so with the dawn of the internet age. Despite sexually explicit content being pigeonholed to the appropriate domains online, the ASMR scene is not exempt from popular culture. Thus, it has seen a stark rise in sexually suggestive content deemed passable by YouTube, but divisive, to put it mildly, within the community.

The line between sensual (ASMR) and overtly sexually suggestive content is seemingly wafer thin. If there is one theme worth taking from this book, it is subjectivity – there is no diktat of tingles, no official guidelines or instructions. Essentially, whatever someone says is ASMR to them is irrefutable. The same principles extend to sexual arousal; it is different for everyone. With this in mind, it makes the sexualisation of ASMR a difficult debate: how can you ascertain the effect a stimulus has on another person or discredit what they know they felt?

A nuanced issue, let's first look at the types of videos that fall within this grey area to understand what could be seen as sexually suggestive. Boyfriend/girlfriend role plays, among others of a similar ilk, have clear romantic, caring connotations, which usually, but not always, focus on the affectionate rather than the physical elements of a relationship. Kissing sounds are increasing in popularity, but, determining if they're intimate or sexual in nature is again uncertain. Usually reserved for female ASMRtists, wearing only a bra or lingerie whilst filming a video has become fashionable for some (yet, I cannot think of a single reason why someone would film an ASMR video in their underwear, if not for the sole, tawdry purpose of inciting a sexual response).

ASMR is believed to be a sensual, intimate and somewhat sensitive experience, with people using it for a farrago of reasons. I would argue that the ASMR response is clearly discernible from a sexual one: the ASMR response isn't clearly limited to defined physical regions (whilst nearly always felt in the scalp/neck regions, it can be felt throughout the body, almost pulsating from the origin, sweeping over the body), yet the experience is routinely described as a euphoric relaxant. The ASMR experience is complex and nuanced; those who experience it and/or engage with the content are motivated by a spectrum of impulses. It is misleading to assume that, as it is a broad experience with somewhat ephemeral borders of definition, by default you can appropriate ASMR as a satellite of sexual fetish. The arousal following sexual experiences is noticeably different. The two responses are priming a person for different behaviours – one that seems to be for relaxation and rest, the other for sexual reproduction. I concede that whilst physically the responses differ, there is an emotional overlap between the two, and that the comfort and intimacy felt by both lead to the blurring between them.

Debating whether sensuality and sexuality are mutually exclusive does little to alter public perception. The reality is that there are fervent acolytes of this new 'sexy' ASMR content, and that wider audiences, if they didn't already find ASMR on the fringes of the taboo already, have noticed this injection of 'kink' into the ASMR formula. Writing in the paper, *'This FEELS SO REAL!' Sense and sexuality in ASMR videos*, Emma Waldron pontificates, 'that through this lens the consumption of ASMR videos can be seen as a sexual practice and the configuration of ASMRtist, viewer-listener, and digital technology can be seen as a sexual relation.' In the clickbait culture we navigate, with gauche video thumbnails depicting censored, 'naked', attractive women, it could be difficult to argue with Waldron's analysis. There is money to made posting ASMR: Lingerie Haul type videos or French Maid Role Plays – the Midas touch of ASMR – so it would be a safe bet to predict more and more videos of a sexual nature flooding the ASMR environment in such a way that it could become the norm, as Waldron would have us believe.

> *'It takes twenty years to build a reputation and five minutes to ruin it'*
>
> **-Warren Buffet**

The proliferation of sexually provocative imagery in nearly all areas of life reflects its integration in our culture. After all, culture is an account of the commonly held beliefs, customs and social behaviour of a society. Quizzically, there is wonderment as to why there is such backlash and disownment of being remotely associated with 'sexual' ASMR among the community, if it is just the somewhat inevitable coalescing of culture.
Those who oppose the changes do so vehemently, with arguments centring on the molestation of ASMR and the tarnishing of an otherwise pure experience. Members of the community feel that if it continues, we will all be tarred with the same brush, that regardless of action, we will all be labelled as producers and partakers of a sexual fetish. Particularly for female creators, the propagation of this style of content wrongly invites lewd, harassing

comments, most egregiously for those who don't even make erotic videos. There is a strong air of stewardship within the community, especially for those who laid the first seeds, who want to cloak ASMR and preserve it. It is hardly unreasonable that those fully committed and involved within the ASMR movement have a keen desire to protect it, bordering on the parental, but that shouldn't be confused with legitimate control. No matter the emotional drive, people have no ownership nor mandate to restrict the interpretation and articulation of ASMR – you cannot dictate a physiological response, for that would be fascism on a biological level.

If there was no defence for this new triggering of ASMR, then the staunchly conservative ASMR community members would retain the status quo of ASMR expression. As you know, there is discord within the community; there are many who counter the anti-sexy arguments and defend this evolution.

The bulwarks argue that it is ridiculous, counterintuitive, and insulting to demand censorship in a group that is imbued with creative freedom and tolerance. ASMR isn't a one-size-fits-all programme; hence, the litany of triggers available to be viewed. Yes, it can be conceded that a portion of the viewers who enjoy the more sexual ASMR do so for transparent, masturbatory motives. Yet, to assume that all who watch it do so for the same reason would be grossly ignorant – and would also be tarring everyone with the same brush, the same sin the opposition complain about. Aside from those who defend 'exotic' ASMR for the sake of liberty, there are those who genuinely have a greater ASMR experience from these videos.

Firstly, they are inherently more intimate, focusing on a direct connection with the participant over the disconnect that arises from blind tapping or other sounds. Secondly, having an ASMRtist appear semi-nude can have the benefit of being disarming; that is, when watching a normal ASMR video, it can be disconcerting to just watch someone whisper at you. So, an imaginary barrier between the viewer and the creator may be erected, diminishing the response. However, as nervous performers are told to imagine the audience in their underwear, the same principle applies – wearing underwear in an ASMR video could enhance a personal connection.

The pseudo-sexualisation of ASMR is essentially an existential crisis –old versus new, the traditional against the contemporary. The opinion I hold on the matter is a conflicted one: I sympathise with those who believe that ASMR is fluid, that someone should not be condemned for trying something risqué. I believe that the beauty of ASMR lies within its quirks, that people should be able to enjoy anything that induces their ASMR – and part of me feels that such outrage for showing cleavage is petulantly prude.

Yet, toiling with the issue further, addressing it from the perspective of a creator, I cannot ignore the uneasiness felt from being remotely associated with something distantly sordid. Whether you create sexualised content or not, your reputation is overridden by the reputation of the genre you align with. To suggest to ASMRtists feeling beleaguered by the changes, 'just don't make sexualised videos' solves nothing. The community is at a crossroads with no sign marking the right path. It has been suggested that sexualised ASMR operate under a similar, but distinct synonym, such as 'SASMR' (S for sexualised) for example, and is an idea that could work, albeit frivolous.

Is it worth it? Is it actually a big deal whether ASMR is seen as sexual?

Again, I believe the answer varies depending on which side of the fence you are on: ASMRtist or viewer. Perhaps taking any action, intervening with the natural development of ASMR's identity, would cause more harm than good. The sexualisation of ASMR is undoubtedly an emerging, fiery debate, a controversial point in its timeline, with a resolution I don't imagine reaching any time soon.

And to be blunt, it doesn't keep me up at night; I firmly believe that the good achieved by ASMR outshines any identity trends it may adopt.

Fake News

For those reading this book who don't experience the effects of ASMR, I imagine levels of scepticism protrude your thoughts. It is hard to explicitly infer the physical reactions that are coveted by those in the ASMR community. As such, you may question whether it truly occurs. As it is only felt by a minority of the population, and with no concrete scientific corroboration, you may view ASMR as pseudoscience. In its current form, our understanding of ASMR is rudimentary, taken at the word of those who claim to experience it, such as myself. Now, while I can proclaim my experience with ASMR is palpable, it is a meaningless statement, and one you have no reason to believe.

In the first part of the book, I briefly mentioned the dissonance that some could feel trying to understand ASMR if they themselves do not feel it. I wanted to address that notion further, focusing on the argument that ASMR is meaningless without proof.

The philosopher Karl Popper, later adapted by Anthony Flew, devised the falsification principle in an attempt to discern what can be classed as meaningful. Flew explored the principle through his allegorical version of the Parable of the Invisible Gardener.

The parable is as follows:

Once upon a time two explorers came upon a clearing in the jungle. In the clearing were growing many flowers and many weeds. One explorer says, 'Some gardener must tend this plot.' The other disagrees, 'There is no gardener.' So they pitch their tents and set a watch. No gardener is ever seen. 'But perhaps he is an invisible gardener.' So they set up a barbed-wire fence. They electrify it. They patrol with bloodhounds. But no shrieks ever suggest that some intruder has received a shock. No movements of the wire ever betray an invisible climber. The bloodhounds never give cry. Yet still the Believer is not convinced. 'But there is a gardener, invisible, intangible, insensible, to electric shocks, a gardener who has no scent and makes no sound, a gardener who comes secretly to look after the garden which he loves. At last the Sceptic despairs, 'But what remains of your original assertion? Just how does what you call an invisible, intangible, eternally elusive gardener differ from an imaginary gardener or even from no gardener at all?'

The meaningfulness of ASMR isn't a corollary to Popper's philosophical enquiry; to adopt Popper's philosophy and conclude that ASMR is meaningless would be a non sequitur. Apart from the obvious difference that the intention of the principle is to apply to an omnipotent, omnipresent deity, it is also based upon the assumption that there exists, or could exist, no empirical data or physical sign of the object in question. Research into ASMR is in its early days, unlike theology, retaining the potential to be neurologically charted. Likewise, it is not inapplicable. The idea of falsification is a useful tool; it is the crux of why some cast aspersions on those proclaiming they experience ASMR. In its current form, ASMR cannot be falsified as only a handful of experiments have been conducted, with no enquiries or metrics as of yet that could possibly conclusively confirm nor deny its existence. You cannot expect blind faith in the testimonies of strangers, with the hope that scientists will shed light on the matter eventually. Fake until proven real.

Stymied once more, the lack of scientific engagement makes the task of convincing non-ASMR experiencers a somewhat insurmountable challenge. Meaningfulness should not be limited to clinical, a posteriori findings as the sole tool for validation. ASMR has impacted the lives of millions, benefiting the way people operate and cope with stressful situations. To label ASMR as pseudoscience is foolish; it is still undecided among the scientific community. I understand the reservation, even dismissal that 'outsiders' may feel, but I remain confident in the community's conviction. When legions of people independently describe the same symptoms, I refuse to reject their experiences, as well as my own, as either a lie or physiological blip.

Cash Cow

The internet age revolutionised business; the dot-com boom inspired a generation of e-commerce titans, including Jeff Bezos (Amazon.com) and Pierre Omidyar (eBay), paving the way for digital marketplaces that require negligible, if any, capital to enter. This generation has seen the birth of 'bedroom billionaires', a term for young, tech savvy and business-minded entrepreneurs. The latest evolution is the social entrepreneur, a person who utilises social-media platforms to earn revenue. YouTube, Instagram and Facebook all offer youthful trendsetters the opportunity to establish their personal empires through advertising revenue and brand sponsorships . . . all they need to provide is the traffic.

ASMRtists are no different; the surge in traffic for ASMR videos has meant that ASMRtists are able to earn sizeable revenue through their content. An ASMRtist can earn revenue through a variety of channels, the most adopted ones being Adsense (Google places adverts over your videos through which you earn a certain rate per thousand impressions) and Patreon (a platform allowing fans to directly contribute to a creator in exchange for tiered rewards). Dedicated fans may even commission private, custom videos featuring their favourite ASMR ingredients. Serious money can be made; it isn't just the YouTube elite that rake in significant earnings. Successful ASMRtists are able to live comfortably off of their hard work – rent, cars and other luxuries are within the grasp of the top whisperers.

The majority of us believe in fair pay for fair work; therefore, it is puzzling why a cluster of people criticise these honest, industrious efforts. Their vitriol labels creators as sell-outs, making suppositions that they are only involved in the community to make money, or that their contributions are fickle, ephemerally jumping on the bandwagon of the latest fad. It is flabbergasting.

These trolls populate a minute, hubristic demographic in the ASMR community that enshrines the sensation in a veil of purity, abusing anyone who doesn't support their perfectionist narrative. A handful of ASMRtists who operate a more erotic channel, do offer explicit videos in exchange for money (further cause for my irresolution regarding sexual ASMR). However, that is no cause for the insults levelled at all those who want to make a sustainable business out of the content that they offer free of charge.

Scarily, the invective spewed isn't sourced solely from some viewers, but even ASMRtists themselves. The internal conflict has always befuddled me; not wanting to commercialise the content that you publish is entirely within your remit, but to criticise others in a vain attempt to impoverish their efforts, just because it doesn't tie in with how you envisaged your hobby, is blatant lunacy. These criticisms are largely ignored and for good reason. I believe that any newcomer to ASMR would not be jarred by the entrepreneurial efforts made by ASMRtists; after all, it is commonplace across all of YouTube.

The ability to convert ASMR from passion to profession is an amazing feat for a group still in its infancy to achieve.

A Tale of Two Beliefs

The real impression I fear a newcomer would have is not that the creators are seen as greedy, or that they are weird, sexual charlatans, but instead that there is a sanctimonious, pompous air to ASMR, a phantom shadow that subtly haunts those involved. An inflated ego underpins moral posturing, gluttonously devouring its laurels whilst deaf and blind to criticism or change. Yet, despite the symptoms of ego universally seen as deplorable, we rarely notice it manifesting itself within ourselves.

Ego and ASMR are by their nature the antitheses of one another. ASMR is built upon tranquillity, acceptance and harmony . . . ego is not. Nature can be deceptive. If you were to remove the rose-tinted goggles and peered closer, you wouldn't have to look far to notice intimations of ego in crevices of the community. Not only in the debates around sexualisation and income, egotism can be found woven into the tapestry of ASMR itself. Take, for instance, the name ASMRtist; we have already discussed the hubris that can be attached to that self-proclaimed title. Even the adoption of the acronym ASMR could be construed as arrogant, using scientific jargon instead of the accessible 'head tingles' when pseudonyms have been used for comparable bodily reactions. Take, for example, goosebumps; hardly anyone knows what the scientific term for that is (FYI it is cutis anserine, catchy!) – is ASMR better than that?

Perhaps I am falling prey to making mountains out of molehills; to accuse the titles used to be egotistical in and of themselves would be woefully contrived. The attention should instead shift to those who are associated with those terms, i.e. the entire ASMR community, and the clash between the easy-going members, happily doing their own thing, unperturbed by others, and the defensive traditionalists. The laidback approach to ASMR is the essence of the community; yet, as we have seen, not everyone is in agreement.

The two behaviours commonly exhibited by the traditionalists are the defensive and founder mentalities. The defensive mentality can be seen as stubborn in its inability to adapt. Those with this mindset in the ASMR community are those who are uncomfortable with triggers or perceptions that they deem embarrassing. Moreover, they are highly sensitive to changes, forcing some (not all) to lash out and rebuke when changes, such as sexual ASMR, arise. The founder mentality is the more overt of the two in terms of capacity for arrogance. The 'founders' are those who were the early pioneers in the ASMR scene, particularly on YouTube for being the original ASMRtists. The incremental moves they made allowed the ASMR movement to pupate; they are revered for their dedication and passion to push through the period when few watched ASMR, roughly pre-2014. The founder mentality can be characterised by a profound sense of responsibility, involvement and quasi-ownership – importantly, the founder mentality doesn't preclude those who joined the community after it was established. Newcomers are still able to mimic those traits (the feeling of ownership, regardless of the date joined, could stem from the intimacy involved and the level of involvement it has in someone's life). Also, the founder mentality does not apply to all who were involved with ASMR in the early days; it is occupied by a very few – a noisy minority. In fact, many of the big players in the ASMR scene today were early maneuverers whose passion and dedication made ASMR relevant today.

The founder mentality has shown itself to be a small, but a potently volatile and ugly presence in the ASMR community. As the community has grown, moving farther in scope from how ASMR began, victims of the founder mentality have become threatened as they feel they are losing the control and influence they once had. Childishly throwing their toys out of the pram, they kick their heels into the dirt, hopelessly resisting the inevitable, attacking the new ASMR hotshots and calling for a return to their hegemony. It is a pity that these few members masquerade their faux self-entitlement as genuine care, a transparent smokescreen for their fragile egos.

Preservation isn't egotistical, and those who prefer the reserved ASMR videos aren't villains. Similarly, the liberals within the community aren't all saints either; they tend to give as good as they take, responding bitterly when they feel threatened. There is no consensus on how to move the community forward, but that shouldn't be an excuse to take it upon yourself, whatever influence you may have, to dictate what should be done. It is the arrogance of the few who are damaging the whole, detracting from the values that shape the community. The internet is big enough for everyone; if you don't like it, close the tab.

Resolution

Writing this segment of the book, I found my opinions wavering as I wrote out my thoughts; forced to look at the arguments from both perspectives, my hesitant conservatism towards ASMR eroded. ASMR is more than a neurological response; it has melded with peoples' lifestyles, ritualistic in their routines. Nothing is perfect, especially something that affects a large body of people in intimate ways, so it is to be expected that discord will arise. All elements that comprise this chapter are pertinent to my life and to those in the ASMR scene. They're debates that we have wrestled with and attempted to tackle. ASMR is weird, wonderful and slightly volatile; that weirdness seeps into misconception, rebellion and denunciation from time to time.

'Healthy scepticism is the basis of all accurate observation'

-Sir Arthur Conan Doyle

ASMR is expanding at an incredible rate. It has no time-weathered traditions, nor entrenched practices; instead, it is malleable and constantly forming. Internal and external criticisms are part and parcel of ASMR. As developments occur, there will be altered opinions, criticisms will be redacted whilst simultaneously new ones will emerge. The divisions within the ASMR community are disheartening, especially as they are conspicuously two sides of the same coin. Arguing in favour of ASMR liberalism or siding with modest ASMR content are parallel paths to the same outcome: recognition, prosperity and acceptance.

The internal clashes, identity crises and other supercilious mishaps will come to define the ASMR culture unless unity is found. The arguments put forward here are trivial compared to the exciting and impactful stories and experiences denoted in previous chapters. Yet, if they persist, the ASMR community may become distracted with dissent, failing its core goal: to stimulate relaxation. Instead, it will become a wretched playground for trolls and remembered as such.

Of the community, 99% are involved for positive reasons, exuding friendship and compatriotism – that is the narrative that does, and should, dominate. The debates I have discussed make up the other 1%, but I believe that it is important to be aware that there can be trouble in paradise. Communities fall out – that is only human. By understanding the differences in opinions, you gain a better insight into the community as a real group of individuals, rather than just the image of the euphoria. Conflict, argument and debate are tools that we are using to build a better community through open dialogue – but that will not force the abdication of connectivity, relaxation and well-being as the driving force of ASMR. They are simply growing pains.

The Long Goodbye . . .

Congratulations, you have made it to the end! No matter the size, I always find finishing a book to be incredibly satisfying, and whilst it has been tremendous fun writing these pages, I can't deny the relief I am feeling as this project draws to a close. I have met and conversed with hordes of interesting characters throughout my time in the community and when gathering resources for this book. The breadth of ASMR culture is immense, given the ostensibly shy size of the community, and whilst interesting, documenting it all would overburden just one book.

With this in mind, I will try the best I can to keep this peroration succinct and free from filibustering.

The intention from the offset was to inform and encourage further discussion and debate around ASMR. That goal has shaped the contents of this book, with the themes chosen specifically to address the questions and queries commonly posed. If you are familiar with the awkward, feeble discussion that occurs when someone asks you off-guard about ASMR, knowing you do not have the time to fully explain, I hope this book proves a useful tool for such encounters. I also truly hope that you take something away from this book. Whether you're involved in ASMR or just curious, ASMR is a complex, but inspiring phenomenon, one I encourage you to at least observe if only out of fascination.

Humans are remarkably complex creatures, and whilst we try to simplify and rationalise our behaviours, nothing is ever as linear as we hope. I have learnt a great deal through writing about the ASMR community; I never before comprehended the vast nuances of sleep, the history that has led to where ASMR is today, nor the extent the platforms have been transmogrified by ASMR. If you began reading with no prior knowledge regarding ASMR, it is hopefully more understandable now why listening to the whispers of strangers has become a nightly routine for many – including myself.

The next time you tuck yourself into bed, wracked with restlessness, staring at the alarm clock with each minute passing feeling like an excruciating eternity, try an ASMR video, even if you're convinced you don't feel the tingling, eponymous phenomenon. What do you have to lose?

What's next?

As certain as night follows day, I believe that the secrets buried under ASMR will be unearthed; the implications of the discoveries, however, are uncertain. Perhaps it will be concluded that it is nothing special, simply a neurological oddity. Perhaps it will continue to gain prominence and popularity, launching the rise of ASMRtists to celebrity status. Perhaps when cracked, it will be used as a respected form of therapy to aid psychologists and psychiatrists, or at least influence a range of sleep-related products.

I expect swathes of people to swell the ranks of the ASMR community; it has already grown rapidly, and with increasing exposure, I believe this is only set to rise. With each addition, new ideas and adaptions will be extolled, pushing the creativity of ASMRtists into new frontiers – adding crazier role plays to the roster. The road is never smooth and issues will certainly arise as ASMR continues to carve its path – but I can guarantee, you will not be finding an ASMR video of myself wearing lingerie . . . no one needs to see that.

ASMR is an island surrounded by the murky waters of ignorance – use this book as a metaphorical lighthouse and explore.

In terms of what you can do next in a more immediate fashion, I have included two additional short sections: ASMR Stories and Becoming a Whisperer. The first is a series of personal ASMR experiences from a variety of folk, showing the ways that ASMR has helped them cope with various obstacles in their lives. Nothing too overwhelming, but a pleasant way to realign with what ASMR is all about – people. The second is more tongue-in-cheek, running you through the steps to become the next whispering sensation . . . it may even become your dream career!

Revolutions have changed the world, be it nationally à la the French or Russian revolutions, or the revolutions of social attitudes, such as those of Martin Luther King Jr. and Nelson Mandela. I am in no way suggesting that ASMR is remotely comparable in significance to these historic events, but to demonstrate the achievements that can be amassed through collective willpower. When human beings come together, rallied by a common motive, nothing big or small is unattainable. For myself, the rest of the community, and perhaps yourself, the ASMR revolution is part of our mark on the world – helping the sleepless sleep one tingle at a time, until restlessness becomes a thing of the past.

Until then, tingle on.

'A conclusion is the place where you get tired of thinking'

-Arthur Bloch

P.S. If you would like to get in contact, I would love to hear your thoughts on the book, but also your own ASMR experiences and your interactions with the community as a whole. Shoot me an email to theasmrgamer00@gmail.com, or find me and my videos online!

ASMR Stories

The ASMR story is nothing without people, it is an intricate web of relationships, connections and tales. Littered throughout the book are insights into the lives of ASMR compatriots, those who contribute and rely on ASMR on a daily basis. I am grateful to all who shared their stories with me, strengthening my resolve for the book, and so I wanted to collate the stories that didn't make it into the main body and share them here:

'Like many others, my ASMR journey began quite by happenstance. For a long time, I used makeup tutorials to fall asleep due to their relaxed nature; one evening, whilst returning to the makeup videos I typically used, I stumbled upon an ASMR makeup video by accident. Discovering that it was more effective than the previous videos I used, I fell down the rabbit hole, continuing to find different types of ASMR such as cranial nerve exam role-plays. Ever since, it has been a reliable tool to help study and unwind!' – Sabrina, USA

'Strangely enough, I discovered ASMR thanks to a video by the YouTubers' Good Mythical Morning; they made a video featuring ASMR which intrigued me, and so I went to check some of it out! I enjoy a few specific ASMR styles: mouth sounds, unintelligible whispering and mukbang. ASMR has had a significant impact on my life, I listen to ASMR every night, almost religiously, as it helps me to sleep – and in all honesty, it makes me feel really good and relaxed.' – Matt, USA

'For as long as I can remember, I have experienced ASMR; I imagined it was something a little strange, meaning I was amazed to see how many others felt the same sensation. Before discovering the community, I would only get ASMR from infrequent and random occasions, but keenly remember the lulling environment of a class helmed by a soft spoken professor. I cannot say that it calms me when I'm angry, nor does it help me fight insomnia – not because ASMR isn't useful, but because when I am stressed I cannot listen to anything, and I rarely ever have sleeping issues. For me, it is another form of relaxation, so when I'm in the mood I put on Gentle Whispering's 3D Tingles.' – Yüksel, Turkey

'I want to say I've always known about ASMR, but until 2015 I was unaware that there was a recognised term for it or that others too experienced it. I stumbled upon ASMR one night when I was looking for tech videos with soothing voices; the search brought up a host of ASMR content and I dove head first into them. The kinds of videos I appreciate the most are soft spoken and whispered role-plays, coupled with my fondness for the U.K accent. ASMR is a tool I use to put myself at ease and calms my mind before sleep.' – Orlando, USA

'I first experienced the tingles of ASMR when I was a kid; I remember feeling so relaxed and my head would tingle as my mother would comb or cut my hair. I never knew what it was or how to describe the feeling because it wasn't well known. A few years ago, I found a cranial nerve exam role-play which brought back the tingling sensation – I couldn't understand why I explored further, watching other ASMRtists. Before finding ASMR, I used to have a hard time sleeping if I was stressed/anxious. Today, my anxiety is not that big a problem because of ASMR, I'm glad ASMR has become somewhat mainstream, but most people I know still don't understand it.' – Greg, USA

'My ASMR eureka moment occurred back in 2015, I was in my room watching a movie when a woman began to speak, creating the ASMR feeling in my head. I had no idea what it was called, but it has happened to me many times before. I found the actual name for it, ASMR, when I searched on YouTube for soft speaking to feel relaxed and the results returned with ASMR. So I typed videogames in front of ASMR and found my favourite ASMR genre! It was an amazing moment, before discovering it on YouTube, I had to get lucky to hear it from people because I didn't know what it was called – I can now relax on demand!' – Tristen, USA

'Before stumbling upon ASMR, I looked for calming music. Instrumentals and soundscapes that would help me to unwind and decompress. Through these searches I stumbled upon videos with the ASMR moniker, videos featuring binaural whispering and light tapping on a variety of objects that sent me into relaxation overload. My serendipitous discovery of ASMR came at the perfect moment, I was bogged down and stressed due to exam season and I found that watching ASMR videos I would calm down and feel more prepared as a result. ASMR is an invaluable tool!' – Addison, England

'I found ASMR because I used to always listen to rain sounds when going to sleep. One of the videos was called ASMR rain sounds, intrigued by the acronym I decided to look it up. So that is how I found it – pleasant coincidence!'

– Michael, Republic of Ireland

'Back when I used to work in retail management a while back I'd sometimes have to work overnight shifts. To decompress when I got home from overnights I'd watch Bob Ross painting videos and have a strong beer or mixed drink before going to bed. I had no idea what ASMR was until I mentioned liking Ross's videos on Twitter; someone suggested I google ASMR and the first official ASMR video I watched was WhisperAudio's makeup video. I loved it. I still watch her videos regularly and have gone on to subscribe to a variety of channels – I now use ASMR to help me get to sleep or if I am editing my photography on the computer.'

– Corey, USA

BENJAMIN NICHOLLS

Becoming a Whisperer

Embarking into the world of ASMR content creation can be a daunting prospect, particularly if you are nervous about appearing in front of a camera or wracked with worry regarding the possibility that friends and family members may find out. If you can overcome those fears then becoming an ASMRtist is incredibly rewarding, in particular the positive impact that you can have on strangers's lives and the community you can build around you. Creating content equips you with technical wherewithal, especially in terms of video production and editing, that is easy to learn as you develop your content, so you shouldn't be dissuaded if you're a complete novice.

ASMR videos range in technicality, but below I have listed the core simple steps that will see you opening your channel, filming your first video, and establishing yourself within the ASMR scene.

Creating Your Channel

Opening your YouTube channel is an incredibly straight forward process requiring you to set up an account and through that account you create your channel(s). But before you begin you should solidify what type of channel you want to run and the corresponding name. In the ASMR community, the names of ASMRtists vary greatly from their own names, creative names involving the ASMR acronym (for example: AndySMR), or more focused on their style of ASMR videos (for example: The ASMR Gamer). You want your channel name to be unique, but not so unique that it becomes confusing. Nomenclature can be tedious, so it is best to pick a name that resonates with you and your personality – don't worry, picking a name isn't the decider of a successful channel and you can always change it later on, although that is discouraged as it can confuse viewers. Once you have picked your name and decided if you are going to tailor your content to a certain ASMR niche then proceed to opening your account and adding the relevant profile picture and channel artwork to further embolden your YouTube persona (tutorials for artwork creation can be found on YouTube).

Filming and Posting Your First Video

When it comes to filming content, newcomers can become bogged down with the high-end cameras and recording equipment that a lot of the bigger YouTubers use. The biggest tip that I can offer you is to just start recording with whatever equipment you have to hand – higher end equipment comes later on, if at all! Modern smartphones already come equipped with impressive cameras and microphones built in meaning there is no need to splash out, simply press record and begin. When I first began creating videos, I created a list of different videos I wanted to create and found this a useful tool, it meant I produced videos quicker as I was working through a list rather than deliberating over what video to make the hour before. Regardless of what videos you create, I suggest you begin with an introduction ramble to introduce your channel and set the scene for your potential subscribers. The video lengths can be what you want them to be, but typically 15+ minutes is a strong target as it offers viewers a substantial relaxation period before having to find another video.

Editing your ASMR videos should be fairly easy unless you are doing green screen work. Basic edits may be required to eliminate any loud disturbances, but by and large your videos will be ready to upload after filming. If you are using a separate audio recorder to the one built in with your camera then you will have to align them in your editing software, but even the most basic editing software, *Windows Movie Maker*, is capable of that. You may want to create an introduction sequence before each of your videos, this isn't particularly common but can help brand your channel and prepare them for relaxation if the sequence is calming.

The next step is uploading the video to your YouTube channel. YouTube gives you lots of tools that you should use to maximise your videos accessibility – you need a clear, enticing title preferably with 'ASMR' thrown in; an attractive custom thumbnail using a screenshot from your video; appropriate, but varied, tags which are keywords that help identify your video and recommend it to potential viewers; and once it becomes available, the correct monetisation settings. The details you input into YouTube are as important as the contents of the video. You need your video descriptors to be honest and inviting if you want to encourage views.

Detailed tutorials for each of these areas of video creating and uploading are available for free online and go into specific tips and tricks. These comments are a brief basic overview to get you going, once you have gotten into your flow and feel more comfortable with the basic knowledge I highly recommend that you read up on more 'specialist' techniques.

Building a Fanbase

No one wants to spend ages creating a high quality video, full of interesting triggers, great title and thumbnail for it to get lost in the YouTube ether. You want to build an audience of voracious viewers that check out all of your videos and leave supportive comments. Building a dedicated horde of fans takes time and effort, but is essential if you want to have your work viewed and for your channel to gain prominence. An easy way to get your name out there in a welcoming community such as ASMR is to demonstrate a genuine interest in the group. This can be done through simply subscribing to and watching ASMRtists you enjoy, commenting on their videos (related to the specific video, not spam channel advertising) and striking conversation. Collaborations are a fun way to introduce different channels to your audience and vice versa, but it is important to remember that asking a much bigger channel to work with you is ill advised and maybe seen as trying to leech off of their success. When I first started creating content, I made it a goal to write genuine comments on five different ASMR videos that had been released that day, and through striking friendships I later collaborated with many channels that I admired.

You don't need to look afield to develop your channel. Focusing on your video quality and output as well as those who already subscribe to you has a big impact on your growth. The YouTube algorithm fluctuates but consistently favours channels who upload frequently, that means if you want to appear in recommended feeds then you want to be uploading at least once a week, but it is much better to be doing so three to four times a week. Frequent uploads also have the added benefit of rewarding your subscribers, you should communicate with your viewers as much as possible, especially in the early days where I made it an objective to reply to every single comment which I was able to achieve until I surpassed 10,000 subscribers. Accept constructive criticism and learn what your audience enjoys and what they don't. You want to treat your viewers highly, showing to passers-by that being a fan of yours is a rewarding experience.

Overview

Pretty much anyone can create an ASMR channel and begin publishing relaxing content. Admittedly some have a more relaxing demeanour by nature, but as long as you enjoy the content you're creating and the people you're interacting with then you're on the right track. Money shouldn't be a motivating factor as the truth is that it takes a while to build a revenue stream and even then it isn't guaranteed to be much if anything. There is a lot more I could go into, for example how to utilise social media and multi-channel networks, but that stuff is too technical for this extra. There is a lot more room in the ASMR sphere for passionate creators, so pick up your camera and film!

See you on there.

REFERENCES

Journals/Books

Barratt, E. Davis, N. (2015). *Autonomous Sensory Meridian Response (ASMR): a flow-like mental state.* PeerJ. University of Swansea

Cytowic, R. Eagleman, D. (2009). *Wednesday Is Indigo Blue.* MIT Press. Massachusetts

Goldschmied, J. et al. (2015). *Napping to modulate frustration and impulsivity: A pilot study.* Personality and Individual Differences

Goller, A. et al. (2013). *Mirror-touch synaesthesia in the phantom limbs of amputees.* Cortex

Huffington, A. (2015). *Thrive: The Third Metric to Redefining Success and Creating a Happier Life.* Harmony. New York City

Maquet, P. et al. (2003). *Sleep and Brain Plasticity.* Oxford: Oxford University Press

Meadows, G. (2014). *The Sleep Book: How to Sleep Well Every Night.* Orion. London

Milner, C. Fogel, S. Cote, K. (2006). *Habitual napping moderates motor performance improvements following a short daytime nap.* Biological Psychology

Popper, K. (1959). *The Logic of Scientific Discovery.* Mohr Siebeck. Germany

Silberman, S. (2009). *The Insomnia Workbook: A Comprehensive Guide to Getting the Sleep You Need*. New Harbinger Publications. California

Simner J, Hubbard EM. (2013). Oxford handbook of Synaesthesia. Oxford: Oxford University Press

Storch, E. et al. (2014). *Misophonia: incidence, phenomenology, and clinical correlates in an undergraduate student sample*. University of Florida

Waldron, E. (2015). *"This FEELS SO REAL!": Sense and Sexuality in ASMR Videos"*. University of California

Articles

http://healthysleep.med.harvard.edu/healthy/matters/consequences

http://dujs.dartmouth.edu/questions/why-do-we-sleep#.Vo2H0hWLShc

http://www.webmd.com/sleep-disorders/features/nix-nightcap-better-sleep

http://www.adaa.org/understanding-anxiety/related-illnesses/other-related-conditions/stress/stress-and-anxiety-interfere

http://psychology.about.com/od/statesofconsciousness/p/TheoriesofSleep.htm

https://sleepfoundation.org/sleep-topics/napping

http://www.apa.org/monitor/2016/07-08/naps.aspx

http://www.sciencedirect.com/science/article/pii/S0191886915003943

https://www.sciencedaily.com/releases/2017/07/170731225418.htm

http://www.dailymail.co.uk/health/article-1092481/Id-hardly-slept-18-months-How-hours-hypnosis-ended-insomnia-nightmare.html

http://technologyadvice.com/podcast/blog/activate-chemicals-gamify-happiness-nicole-lazzaro/

http://www.experienceproject.com/stories/Have-Asmr/2595472

http://www.mdjunction.com/forums/4s-selective-soft-sound-syndrome-discussions/general-support/10408342-misophonia-and-asmr

http://hudsonoriginals.com.au/?gclid=Cj0KEQiA_MK0BRDQsf_bsZS-_OIBEiQADPf--vX62Sqv_10VUkDQQqVO09ashLexIT-ttvGS5jCiWNkaAmXT8P8HAQ

https://www.reddit.com/r/misophonia/comments/2rta0k/trigger_warning_misophonia_and_asmr/

http://theunnam3df33ling.blogspot.co.uk/2010/07/theory-is-asmr-actually-type-of.html

http://www.mind.org.uk/information-support/types-of-mental-health-problems/post-traumatic-stress-disorder-ptsd/#.VpbTthWLShc

http://www.combatstress.org.uk/medical-professionals/what-is-ptsd/

https://www.myptsd.com/c/threads/asmr.26507/

http://metro.co.uk/2015/10/21/soothing-asmr-helped-my-stress-and-insomnia-so-now-i-make-videos-that-give-others-braingasms-5452605/

https://www.reddit.com/r/asmr/comments/1i87wm/

https://www.health.harvard.edu/mind-and-mood/mindfulness-meditation-practice-changes-the-brain

https://www.britannica.com/topic/Buddhism/Historical-development#toc68669

http://www.vice.com/read/asmr-the-good-feeling-no-one-can-explain

http://www.steadyhealth.com/topics/weird-sensation-feels-good

https://groups.yahoo.com/neo/groups/sos_08/info

http://theunnam3df33ling.blogspot.co.uk/2010/02/welcome-to-unnamed-feeling-aka-tingling.html

https://www.leeds.ac.uk/news/article/4079/insufficient_sleep_could_be_adding_to_your_waistline

https://www.sleepio.com/2012report/

http://science.sciencemag.org/content/306/5702/1776

http://plumbingthedepths.tumblr.com/post/48371458135/intp-and-autonomous-sensory-meridian-response

https://www.surveymonkey.com/r/MFJ5ZPG

https://www.infjs.com/threads/asmr-anyone-into-it.23305/

http://personalitycafe.com/member-polls/117646-mbti-asmr.html

ACKNOWLEDGMENTS

I'd like to thank the ASMR community as a whole for their support during this project. Whenever I was tired or stressed, the ASMR community would be waiting for me with just a few clicks of the cursor. It is truly the best community in the world.

I want to thank Dr. Richard for embarking on this task with me. Despite the time it has taken, he was always willing to lend a hand – or a word or two. Without said help this book would be half as long and only a fraction as good.

I want to thank my parents, sisters, and the rest of my family for encouraging me to pursue a whisper based business and all the opportunities it has provided despite the unsociable hours it demands.

THE AUTHOR

Benjamin Nicholls is an entrepreneur and budding author. He started his digital content business at age 16 and continued to grow his audience on three different platforms where he receives 100,000s of views per month. Passionate about relaxation, technology, and marketing, Benjamin strives to combine these passions to entertain and inform, primarily, about the ASMR phenomenon.

Benjamin is also the author of:

How To: Grow Your YouTube Channel in Six Easy Steps – an eBook focused on the six pillars of a successful YouTube career.

ASMR: THE SLEEP REVOLUTION

Made in the USA
Las Vegas, NV
16 April 2021